RAMBL

IN THE
COTSWOLDS

22 walks covering 250 miles

Peter Drinkwater

&

Harry Hargreaves

First published by
Thornhill Press
24 Moorend Road
Cheltenham

© Peter Drinkwater and Harry Hargreaves
1981

2nd edition 1987

ISBN 0 946328 18 8

The maps are based upon the relevant Ordnance Survey maps with the permission of the Controller of Her Majesty's Stationery Office, Crown Copyright reserved.

Typeset by Wessex Typesetters
(Division of The Eastern Press Ltd)
Frome, Somerset

Printed by
The Eastern Press Ltd
Reading and London

Authors' Note

It is a few years since our first book of Cotswold rambles was published. Inevitably, in the course of time, variations are made in fields and woods and to tracks and paths. A need for revision of the book was desirable and also experience has shown that more precision could be given to some of the narrative which would enable the rambler to follow without any hesitation.

The book did, we are assured, serve a useful purpose. We have however as a result of a good deal of pleasurable walking and observation over subsequent years, felt that we could make a book of much wider scope to cover other areas in the Cotswolds, some of which are not well known, although they are of great charm and interest. Meanwhile Harry Hargreaves' *Cotswold Rambles* (£1.95) is still available as also is his *Second Book of Cotswold Rambles* (£1.95).

Some of the 22 rambles in this book will, we think, make the rambler aware of some parts of the Cotswolds which he would otherwise miss. We know they can all be walked with enjoyment.

We appreciate the debt we owe to those Clubs and Authorities who have contributed to the keeping open and protection of the countryside. Special mention must be made of the Evesham Rambling Club, The Ramblers Association and especially the Gloucestershire Section, The Cotswold Wardens, The Commons Open Spaces and Footpaths Preservation Society, The National Trust and the Countryside Commission. We wish to record our appreciation of the co-operation we have received from the Footpaths Section of the Gloucestershire County Council in providing facilities for the examination of maps and seeking the removal of obstructions.

On a personal basis, we should like to thank all those ramblers and especially the members of Evesham Rambling Club who have walked with us and added to our enjoyment; and also Max Lovatt who took the photographs.

Finally, all those who have directly or indirectly been interested in the production of this book are very appreciative of the many farmers who have been helpful in removing obstructions and have co-operated in the clearance of footpaths.

August 1987
Peter Drinkwater
Harry Hargreaves

The Country Code

Please remember, as you walk through the countryside, to respect the privacy and livelihood of those who live in the country. The Country Code asks you to:

1. Guard against all risk of fire
2. Fasten all gates
3. Keep dogs under proper control
4. Keep to paths across farmland
5. Avoid damaging fences, hedges and walls
6. Leave no litter
7. Safeguard water supplies
8. Protect wild life, plants and trees
9. Go carefully on country roads
10. Respect the life of the countryside

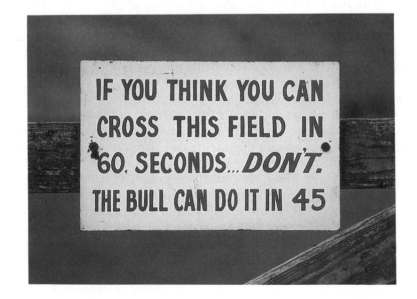

INTRODUCTION

This book contains approximately 255 miles of rambling. The shortest ramble is 7 miles and the longest 17 miles. The area covered is from Mickelton in the north to Miserden in the south, an area of unlimited charm and interest in which one is spoilt for choice. The narrative is so detailed that it is hoped that each ramble can be followed without reference to a map. Nevertheless the map at the beginning of each ramble should enable the rambler to pinpoint his position, and, if lack of concentration or another interest has involved a deviation from the walk, it will enable him to get back to the narrative. In addition many ramblers may wish to understand the ramble in relation to the surrounding area; therefore the appropriate Ordnance Survey map 1/50000 scale (approximately 1¼″ to the mile) applicable to each ramble is stated at the beginning.

At the beginning of each ramble a place is named which is on the map on the back of the book. From the place named the ramble begins or a description is given how to get to the starting point from the place. It is stating the obvious to say—*Make sure you get the right starting point.*

Each ramble starts and finishes at the same place.

Allow at least one hour for each 2 miles of rambling.

Whilst the Cotswolds do not have the dangers of mountains or wild moorlands some precautions will ensure that enjoyment is not marred. Therefore make sure your clothing and especially your footwear is comfortable and adequate, and see that you have sufficient time to complete the ramble before sunset.

Whilst every endeavour has been made to ensure that each ramble follows throughout its length the existing Rights of Way, and every possible care has been taken to ensure the accuracy of all information in the book, the Authors and Publisher cannot accept any liability for the accuracy of the information given or for its interpretation by readers.

Index

Ramble 1
MISERDEN, EDGEWORTH, RIVER FROME, VALLEY FARM

Some excellent hilly walking with fine views.
Map O.S. 163 in the 1/50000 series.
Starting point: Grid reference 937089 Village of Miserden.
Distance 7 miles. Miserden is to the west of the A417(T) about 6 miles
north of Cirencester

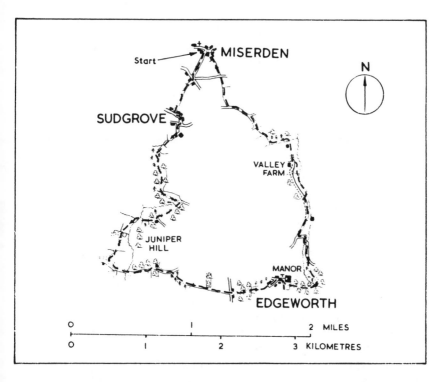

From the shelter in the centre of the village, go up the road with the
Carpenter's Arms on the right. At the road junction turn left towards
Edgeworth. In 40 yards turn right along a public footpath. In a few
yards pass through a kissing gate and continue along a green track to a
road. Turn left. At the next road junction, where there is a Post Office
letter box, turn sharp right. Go down and take the first turn to the left.
Just before the first farm building go over the stone stile on the right.
Follow the fence on the left. About 25 yards before the fence turns to
the right, cross it and the tiny brook and continue near the fence now
on the right. The way is down a rough area following the line of the

fence, through brambles and crossing a stream where it falls over a steep bank. From here walk about 45 degrees to the right to a bridle gate leading into the wood. The path in the wood curves to the left and climbs a steep and slippery bank but levels out into a green track. Follow this and pass through a gate. About 220 yards from the gate look carefully for a very narrow and indistinct track on the right which descends steeply to the bottom of the bank. Carry on until the track swings sharply to the left by a cottage. 25 yards before this cottage leave the main track and go down a path so leaving the cottage to the left. Descend for about 250 yards.

At the bottom of the descent, as the path leaves the trees, the view opens out across the valley and on the skyline can be seen the spire of Bisley Church. The path descends to a gate by the stream but the gate is wired up. Ten yards to the left, however, there is a stile and a stepping stone across the stream. Immediately after crossing the stream turn left and follow the stream to the end of the field: turn right for about 50 yards to a small gate. Go through the gate, cross a stream and turn right to ascend towards a clump of beech trees. On arriving at a path turn left. This leads to a gate and another bridged stream. Follow the main track for over 200 yards to a clear main track. Turn left downhill. Almost at the bottom of the hill there is a gate on the right; avoid this and continue ahead (often along a shallow stream) to another gate. Pass through this gate and do not take the obvious track to the right but continue straight ahead for 30 yards, pass over the stile on the left and loop round and, in about 150 yards, pass through another gate on to the original track. Keep to this track which in about 200 yards turns sharply left uphill. Where another track comes in from the right go through the gate ahead (at the time of writing the gate was removed and only a gap in the wire remained). Follow the main track passing to the right of some foresters' buildings. In 100 yards enter the wood on the right up a green track emerging by a gate into a field.

Follow the hedge on the right down the side of this field, cross the road and take the track opposite between two cottages (or gate-houses). Where the track forks keep to the right and go downhill through the gate towards a house just visible in the valley.

Pass under some power cables strung on poles. In about 150 yards fork left to pass through a gate by a cottage (South Lodge Cottage) into the lane. Continue straight ahead, with the church on the left, to face the Manor House in Edgeworth.

Just before the Manor gates take a green track on the right. It gives the impression of being private ground but it is a public right of way. This leads to a bridge. On the other side go up the track to the road. Turn left down the hill and cross the stream. At the second left hand bend on the hill turn right signposted 'Valley Farm'. Go ahead and cross a cattle grid and in 400 yards from the Valley Farm sign referred to and 30 yards before a second cattle grid there are two gates on the right. Go through the first and descend to the bottom of the valley. Turn left and in about 500 yards a fence is arrived at across the valley. Here bear left and pass through a field gate in this fence. Go ahead along the contour of the hill gradually rising to the left making for a gate just beyond Valley Farm but at a point where there is a cottage adjacent to Valley Farm and a farm track. Valley Farm is immediately on the left with the interesting outline of an old wood fired oven and a marvellous roof. Please do not go towards the farm which is a private residence but turn right. Pass through one gate and then another and then to the right of a cattle shed so as to come to a facing fence. A few yards to the left is a stile over barbed wire. Cross this and turn left keeping close to the fence on the left for about 200 yards to a gate. Do *not* go through the gate but turn right up a rough steep slope, keeping close to the wire and crossing a stile at the top into a field. Keep the hedge on the left and leave this field by the stile next to the left hand gate. In 30 yards go through an open gateway, the wire fence and hedge now being on the right.

The track leads into a green lane by a belt of trees. Where two lots of power lines cross each other turn right through a broken gateway and keep the stone wall on the left to a road. Cross and go down the track opposite with the wall of Great Miserden Park on the right. At the end of the field go over a stone stile and the track passes between two stone walls into Miserden and the beginning of the walk.

Ramble 2
WINCHCOMBE, SALTERS HILL.
LITTLE FARMCOTE, LYNES BARN,
SUDELEY LODGE, WINCHCOMBE

A delightful short walk.
Map O.S. 163 in the 1/50000 series.
Starting point: Grid reference 025282 Winchcombe.
Distance 8 miles.

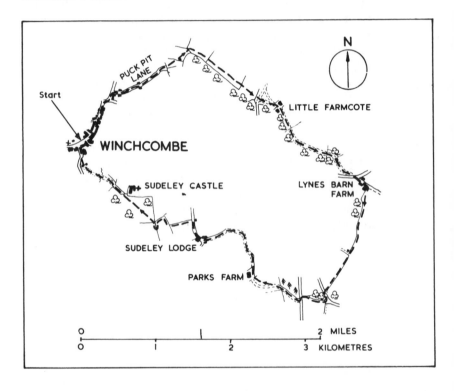

From the car park in the centre of Winchcombe walk along the A46 so as to leave the Methodist Church and the George Hotel on the right. Continue down the hill and over the stream and take the second turn on the right at a house called Hayles Way. This lane is called Puck Pit Lane. Follow the lane bearing right at a signpost Hailes Abbey 2 km. Continue along this lane which becomes a track and finishes at the entrance to a field which has a post at the entrance on the left with the Cotswold Way sign. Go diagonally left across this field towards an old barn with a corrugated iron roof. Just preceding the barn there is a gate on the left with a Cotswold Way sign. Go through and turn right to pass the barn which is now on the right. Just past the barn turn left along a green track and with a hedge on the right continue to the end of the field. Turn left for about 25 yards. Go through a kissing gate on the right. Turn diagonally right to a line of trees and ascend with these trees to the right. Continue to and go through a gate. Ignore a stile which is a few yards to the right. Continue ahead with the trees to the right. When the line of trees finishes continue towards a clump of trees on a knoll. At the foot of the knoll go through a gate in the facing wall. Go in the same direction across the next field to a gate and on to a road which is the Salt Way. Go down the track immediately opposite and on through Little Farmcote farmyard.

Rise up slightly to the right to follow the lower edge of a rough wood for 1 mile passing at one place through a small extension of the wood to emerge on the road at Lynes Barn. Turn left and at the fork go right. In 150 yards at the end of the buildings, turn right into the first field to follow the edge of a wood up and round to the left. Continue with the hedge on the right to the disused cottages near Farmcote Wood Farm. The track to the farm is on the right but continue ahead with the hedge on the left to the road. Turn left for 100 yards. Turn right at a rough parking space and continue along a track for only a few yards. Go through the first opening on the right to follow the edge of the wood, which is on the right, and then a wall to the road. Turn left and in 20 yards turn right through a bridle gate. Follow the track down to Parks Farm. On arriving at the rear of the farm turn right and follow the same contour on to the farm road. Go down the road to Sudeley Lodge.

After passing through the yard of Sudeley Lodge continue along the drive to the end of the field on the left where there are two houses on the right. Go through the wicket gate on the left and follow the hedge which is on the right to the corner. Go over the waymarked stile. Turn right and walk for 150 yards to the corner of the field. Turn left and follow the hedge for 200 yards to the corner. Go over the waymarked stile and bear immediately right and pass over the stile and tiny brook.

Bear diagonally left to Sudeley Castle. Go to the left of Sudeley Castle to a kissing gate. Keep to the left of a children's playground to another kissing gate. Do not enter the playground. Follow the fence enclosing the playground and pass through another kissing gate. Continue ahead to an estate road. Follow the road down to a lodge and go through the kissing gate on the left. Continue ahead to the road in Winchcombe.

Ramble 3
EVENLODE AND LITTLE COMPTON

Maps O.S. 151 & 163 in the 1/50000 series.
Starting point: Grid reference 225290 Evenlode.
Distance 8 miles.

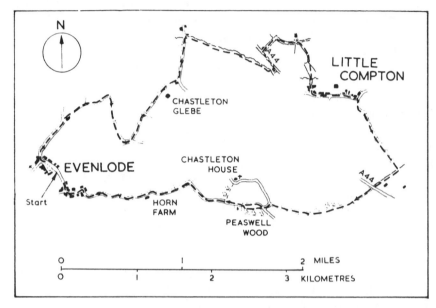

Start at the village green with the old school (now a private house) on the right. Walk along the road and bear right at the signposted Moreton-in-Marsh road for ½ mile. Where the road curves left leave it to follow a good farm road ahead (with a sign indicating it is not a through road). Follow this for nearly ¼ mile and at the sharp left bend go forward through a gate. Follow the hedge on the right across two fields and in the right hand corner of the second field turn right and go through the gate.

Follow the hedge on the left over two fields and pass through a gate into a track with hedges on both sides. In 25 yards turn left to follow a narrower track for ½ mile.

Cross a stream and pass through a gate and go ahead with a hedge on the right to pass through the field into a wider track between hedges. At the metalled drive bear slightly right and pass the entrance to Chastleton Glebe.

At the road near the lodge turn left. In ¼ mile there is a bridge with white wooden rails. Immediately before this turn into the meadow on the right and follow the stream.

14

In ¾ mile the back of a garage can be seen through the trees to the left. Cross the stream by a footbridge and follow the waymarks to the main road A44.

Turn left. In about 100 yards turn up the bridleway on the right which is quite a good farm road. In less than ½ mile follow round to the right. In about a further 200 yards there is a house on the right and Salters Well Farm on the left.

Continue straight ahead along an indefinite grass track. In about 70 yards there is a gate straight ahead. Do *not* go through this but turn right for 40 yards and go through the gate into a field.

Follow the hedge which is on the right. In about 200 yards the hedge turns right, continue to follow it as it descends. About 80 yards before the bottom of this field go through the hedge into the adjoining field.

From here descend diagonally right to the bottom right hand corner of the field. Go over the fence and then over a bridge and walk along the green track past the Red Lion Inn to the main road.

Here turn left through the village of Little Compton.

In ½ mile where the road curves sharply left a bridleway sign stands opposite pointing through a gate on the right.

Follow the hedge which is on the left uphill for ½ mile to a gate in a stone wall. Do not go ahead but turn right along a good track on the edge of the quarry and so to the A44.

Cross the road and walk along the lane opposite across Chastleton Hill, much of which is parkland, for nearly a mile. This road now crosses a cattle grid on to a country lane. Turn left and in 100 yards where the road turns sharply left, turn right into a narrow track into a wood. In 25 yards the track forks. The track to the right is a non-maintained road. Follow this as it curves down to the left through Peaswell Wood to a gate into Chastleton Park.

Go ahead with the wood on the left for 300 yards to a gate which leads to a track between two hedges. This track curves downhill for nearly ½ mile.

On crossing the stream at the bottom of the hill turn left and follow the stream through four fields to pass Horn Farm. Continue along the good farm road into Evenlode.

At the junction in the village turn right to the start and completion of the walk.

Ramble 4
WILLERSEY TO CHIPPING CAMPDEN

A walk over hills connecting two typical Cotswold villages and including Dover's Hill, a National Trust Property.
Map O.S. 151 in the 1/50000 series.
Starting point: Grid reference 105396 Village of Willersey.
Distance 9 miles.

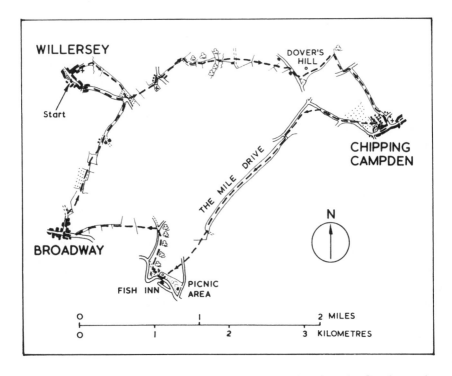

Follow the road opposite the pool as far as the church. Go through a gate into the churchyard and take a path on the left. Pass over a stile in the wall on the left and turn right. Keeping the wall and then the hedge on the right, continue to a point in the facing hedge 15 yards from the corner of the field. Go over a stile and stone footbridge into a field. Continue through the field up the hill keeping a hedge on the left, crossing one stile as far as a cherry orchard. Enter the cherry orchard over a stile. Bear right away from the hedge on the left to a road gate. Do not go through the gate but turn left before it back to the hedge just left to the double stile over a brook. (This seems circuitous but it follows the right of way.) Cross the stiles and follow the path across a field towards Saintbury church seen ahead. Aim slightly to the left of the church. At the church go to the left of the field and pass over the stile. Immediately turn right to the church path, thus avoiding the private drive. Descend along the church path towards the village.

On reaching the road turn right for 30 yards to a small barn on the left. Take a path on the left of the barn and enter a field over a stile. Keep a hedge on the left and some farm buildings on the right to enter the next field. Follow the fence which is on the left. There is a small gate on the left and 10 yards past it a large field gate. Go through the latter and turn right, keeping alongside the hedge which is on the right. Take the first gate on the right and enter a green lane with a wire fence on the right and bushes and trees on the left. In 100 yards go over the stile on the left of the gate. In a few yards pass over another stile into another field. Follow the trees and fence which are on the left and pass through a gate into the next field. Continue with trees and fence on the left. Ignore a gate on the left and descend to a gate in the bottom left hand corner of the field. Pass through the gate and cross the brook and in a few yards go over the stile ahead to the left of a field gate. Follow the hedge which is on the right. Go over the stile in the corner and cross the footbridge into a large field.

Ascend to the right to cross a farm track at a point where there is a footpath signpost. Follow the direction indicated by the signpost to the stile in the top right hand corner. Bear slightly left so as to arrive at a facing fence about 100 yards to the right of a farm. Go over the signposted stile. Walk straight ahead ascending the field to a hedge. Turn left and pass over the stile in the corner of the field to the road.

Turn right up the road past Foxborough Farm on the right, and enter Dover's Hill by a kissing gate on the left with a National Trust sign. Follow the line of trees to near the top of the hill but just before the top bear left to the topograph.

Bear left round the rim of the hill. At the trig. point bear right to a stile in the right hand hedge with a Cotswold Way sign giving access to a field. Go over a stile and follow the fence and hedge on the left to the road at a signpost "Dover's Hill, Aston Subedge 2 km." Turn left on the road and in a few yards turn right down the bridle road with the sign "Chipping Campden 1 km." Descend towards Chipping Campden. Bear right at a sign "Hoo Lane, Cotswold Way" and enter the main street of Chipping Camden. Four miles have now been walked. (The main part of the town is on the left.)

Turn right in the main street. Go up the first turn on the right marked "Littleworth" into a new estate. Turn left into a short drive opposite a "No cycling" notice. Enter a field and go diagonally right as indicated by the footpath signpost. Go over the stone stile to the road by a signpost "Public footpath Chipping Campden". Turn right up the road. Avoid the private drive on the left.

Turn left into a field at a sign "Public footpath Broadway Tower". Follow the line of the sign to the left of a lone tree in the field, to a gap in the bank by the road. Remain in the field close to the bank on the right. Leave the field by a stone stile or gap and turn left into a short drive with a Cotswold Way sign. Just before reaching a gateway turn right through a gap in the wall and continue along a broad avenue known as "The Mile Drive". This drive in the 18th century was a great horse racing place. When George IV was Prince of Wales he regularly attended races here and stayed at Farncombe House. In about one mile there is a cartway going off on the left with a notice that there is no right of way. At this point leave the drive through the facing stone wall with a Cotswold Way sign. Cross the field to a stone stile 50 yards from the left hand corner. In the next field go diagonally right to the corner of the field and through a gap on to the road. Turn left to the sign on the right "Broadway Hill 1.5 km, Broadway 3 km." Follow the direction of the sign across a field aiming for the right hand end of the buildings on the horizon.

Go over the stile in the fence and walk to the right of the topograph to a signpost and follow the direction "Woodland Walk" and enter the nature reserve. Follow the footpath to the right. Descend some steps with a waymark. At the bottom of the descent turn right and continue following the waymarks. Go up some steps and at the top continue for a few yards to a signpost. Turn right the signpost saying "Broadway". Go along the ridge and then descend some steps to the road. Cross the road and go over the stile with a signpost. Walk northwards so as to descend with a fence to the right. Veer away from the fence so as to be 100 yards to the left of it on arriving at the facing hedge, where there is a stile.

Having crossed the stile continue the descent in the same direction making for a point where a hedge from the right makes a junction with a hedge continuing the line of descent. Walk on with the latter hedge on the right to a gate: pass through and follow the track to an open field and then continue with a fence and hedge on the left to another gate. Go through the small gate and then over the stile immediately in front.

Continue with the fence on the right to the main road A44.

Turn right down the road towards Broadway. In about 150 yards turn right into a lane beside Knap House (signposted Willersey/ Saintbury Church). The lane becomes a farm track. Where the track forks, before the drive to Hill Farm, turn right through a wicket gate. Go through the wicket gate seen ahead. Continue in the same direction to a fence. Turn left and follow the fence. When the fence is followed by some trees and a scrub fence and about 50 yards from the corner of the field, bear slightly left and in a few yards go over a stone slab and stile fence to enter an orchard. Follow the hedge which is on the right.

18

The hedge takes a right angled turn but continue ahead in the same direction with the hedge still on the right. Go over a stile and a stone bridge to enter an open field. Follow a hedge which is on the right and pass over a stile into a field with the buildings of a security organisation seen ahead. Walk to the right of a large tree to a gap in the hedge on the right with a footpath sign. On going through the gap in the hedge turn left. Go through the car park and continue straight ahead along the drive to the road.

Either turn down the road into Willersey or cross the road and enter the orchard through the gate opposite and bear left through the orchard, thus rejoining the earlier part of the walk and returning to Willersey church.

Broadway Tower

19

Ramble 5
SNOWSHILL HILL, BLOCKLEY, DOVEDALE WOOD, BOURTON DOWNS

A pleasant easy walk taking in the Dovedale Woods and the Bourton Downs.
Maps O.S. 150 & 151 in the 1/50000 series.
Starting point: Grid reference 108331.
Distance 9½ miles.

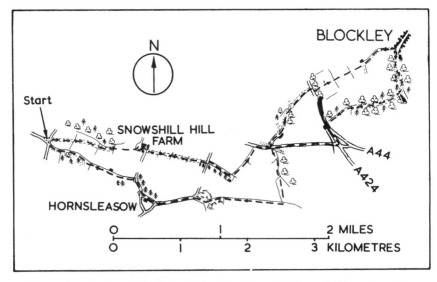

To get to the starting point take the Snowshill road from Broadway. On entering Snowshill bear left so as to leave the church on the right. Continue ahead over two minor cross roads to the T-junction which is ¾ mile from Snowshill.

This is the starting point.

At this T-junction turn left (signposted Bourton-on-the-Hill 4½ miles, Morteon in Marsh 6¾ miles). In 75 yards take the well defined grass bridle track on the right across four fields without deviation to reach Snowshill Hill Farm.

With a wall enclosing the farmhouse on the right, continue straight ahead through the farm and pass through a gate into a bridle road. Follow the bridle road across four fields direct to a road via a gate at the entrance to Smallthorns Farm. Turn left for 35 yards, then right for ¼ mile to Bourton Far Hill Farm. Pass through a gate at the approach to the farm and after a few yards, with the farmhouse on the right, turn left through a gate and follow a wall on the left. Continue through 2 gates before descending to a gate on to the road; turn right for 200 yards, then turn left at the entrance to Far Upton Wold. Follow this roadway to the Jockey Stable Cottages. Near the last cottage, on the right, cross over the cattle grid, turn sharp right for a few yards then sharp left.

Continue ahead across the field with a stream on the left towards the woods ahead. Go past a pond which is on the left towards a wall enclosing the wood. Carry on with the wall on the right and pass through two gates to join a bridle road which ascends to the main road A44.

Cross the road turn right and in 20 yards take the bridle track on the left passing through a coppice fringing the road. In 30 yards enter an open field. Cross this field with the hedge on each side about equidistant away, making for an opening in the fence on the other side, the opening being about 150 yards from a wood on the left. Go through the opening and follow the farm track and descend to Warren Farm.

A definite farm track now leads to a road coming in from the left. Continue ahead to a road and turn left into Blockley which offers a choice of two inns. (4 miles have now been walked).

From Blockley, walk back along the road just traversed (past the point at which the cart track joined the road) to enter Dovedale, where the metalled road merges into a cart track with woodland on each side. Follow this well-defined track past the pumping station, and with Bourton Wood on the left, without deviating, until it joins the Five Mile Drive A44 at Trooper's Lodge. Here turn left. At the junction of A44 and A424 go along A424 for about 200 yards, and at the first cross roads turn right. In about ¾ mile nearly at the bottom of the descent and a few yards before a road on the right, which goes to Far Upton Wold, go through a signposted gate on the left. Follow the track with a fence on the right and ascend the field. At the top go through a gate on the right to enter a coppice. On emerging from the coppice follow the bridleway markings alongside a hedge which is on the left. In about 150 yards a bridleway marking points up the field to the right. Go in this direction to the top right hand corner of the field, pass through a bridle gate and then follow the hedge which is on the right to a farm track; turn right. Follow the track alongside a wall and then a hedgerow across Bourton Downs. The track descends past a stone quarry (on the right) and then goes through a wicket gate into a field of shrubs. Here an ill-defined footpath follows a hedgerow and after a few yards descends steeply through the bushes on the right. Immediately before another wicket gate at the bottom of the slope, the path goes through the bushes on the right and leads on to the road. Bear left and follow the road for about ¼ mile and just prior to the first major bend to the left, leave the road and pass through a gate on the right. Follow the cart track past Hornsleasow Farm on the left to join a metalled road. Continue along the road to the end of the conifer plantation bordering the right hand side of the road.

At a point where the road begins to ascend, just before a small stone building, turn off the road through a gate on the left to join a bridle track running alongside a wall which is on the right. When the track forks continue straight ahead, still keeping alongside the wall on the right. Pass through a gate and continue ahead with a wood on the left, and still with the wall on the right. At the end of the wood go through a gate, and, still following the wall continue along the bridle track to the road and the completion of the ramble.

By Snowshill

Snowshill

Ramble 6
WINCHCOMBE, LANGLEY HILL, NOTTINGHAM HILL, WOODMANCOTE

A walk over 3 hills with good views over Winchcombe and Cheltenham.
Map O.S. 163 in the 1/50000 series
Starting point: Grid reference 025282 Winchcombe.
Distance 9½ miles.

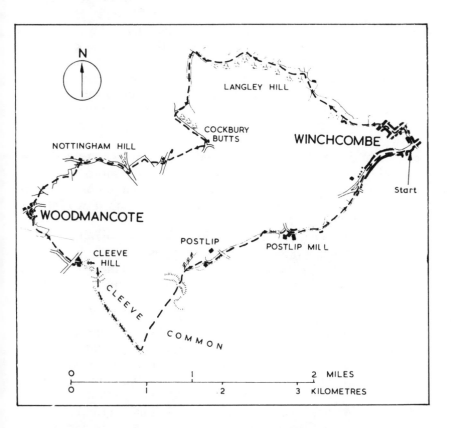

From the car park in the centre of Winchcombe turn right along the road to Broadway and then immediately turn left up the lane opposite the Methodist Church. In about 200 yards, take the footpath on the left and at a junction with the road turn left. (New Library and Clinic on the left). Take the second road on the right, Barnmeadow Road, and go to the end to the T-junction. Here turn left up Orchard Road and at the end of the road turn right and take the footpath signposted "Langley Hill 1 mile".

23

Go over the stile and cross the field towards the farm buildings seen ahead. Pass through a gate and continue towards the farm buildings. Just before the buildings veer right to a stile. Go over this and the tiny brook. Bear left uphill. There are two gates ahead. Take the left hand one and continue in the same direction up the hill to the top of the field. Go over the stile in the top right hand corner with a Wychavon Way mark; a yellow W and an arrow.

Continue ahead to the wall opposite, turn left, and follow the track with the wall on the right. A short way along this track there are two tracks sharp to the left which go to the summit of Langley Hill but the walk is straight on. On reaching a fork, the right hand of which goes to a gate giving access to a field, take the left hand definite track and carry on along this track following the Wychavon Way signs immediately below the wooded slopes on the left. Pass through a gate and still follow the signs but 60 yards before a bridle gate leave the Wychavon Way and pass through this gate. Still keep the wood on the left for ¼ mile over rough ground and at the end of the wood go 200 yards to the stone wall.

Bear right downhill along a fence and a line of trees. At the bottom of the field go through a gate on the left. Go ahead (ignore the gate on the left) for 60 yards to another gate. Pass through into a track with trees on both sides and a fence on the left. On arriving at two gates go through the right hand one.

Where the trees finish on the left follow a fence on the right for a few yards to a gate which pass through, veer slightly left and in 30 yards pass through another gate. Now follow the hedge on the left to a small barn under some power lines. Immediately turn right to descend the field with a fence to the right.

Go through the bridle gate at the bottom of the field. Turn left and walk with a wood on the left. When the wood ends go through a gate and continue in the same general direction over two fields towards a house. Near the house go through a gate on the left on to the road.

Turn right and in 30 yards go over the fence on the right. This brings the walker into the same field just left but the description follows the right of way. Walk up the field towards the left hand group of houses on the sky-line crossing a fence and a 5-bar gate in the intervening hedges. Pass through a single gate on to the track immediately in front of a pair of cottages and turn left. Almost immediately turn right through a gate and follow the hedge on the right to the corner. Cross the wall (it is easier to go to the gate in this wall but it is not the right of way) and bear left to about half way along the left hand wall. Go over this wall and turn right and follow the wall. At the corner turn left and follow this wall to its junction with a track. Cross the stone stile, turn left, and at the road turn right downhill. At the bottom of this hill go past Longwood Farm. In a further ⅓ mile there is a house on the right obscured in vegetation and which precedes a descent of the road; this is about 5 yards before a road sign indicating that the road narrows. Here go over the stone stile on the left and go straight ahead over another stone stile. In 20 yards at the corner turn right. Go slightly left to a wooden stile. Keep the same direction for 50 yards then bear right to the stone stile at the bottom of the field. Bear slightly left across a field to go through a gate. Turn left and go over a wooden fence. Turn right and then descend through bushes and trees to Woodmancote at the Apple Tree Hotel car park and so to the road. Refreshments are available at the Apple Tree Hotel. (5½ miles have not been walked).

Turn right out of the car park and take the first road left (Hillside Gardens) beyond the Free Church. Turn right at the T-junction and take the path in the left corner between the houses. Cross the stile and bear left uphill with a line of willow trees just to the right. Cross the next wooden fence and continue uphill in the same direction towards the Rising Sun Hotel at the top.

Cross the stile in the right hand corner of the field, go over the main road and up the road opposite on the right of the Rising Sun Hotel. Go straight ahead over several main cross paths. In a few yards pass to the left of a small plantation of trees. In a further 100 yards pass to the left of another small plantation. The path merges into a stony track coming uphill from the right. In 15 yards follow this track round to the right. Continue ahead with the golf course on the left and Cheltenham ahead and below on the right in the valley.

At a point where 5 paths meet, continue ahead taking the left hand fork. (If this point is mised the way will be picked up by going in the same direction). Soon the radio masts will be seen ahead. A little beyond the 13th tee, there is a single tree in a circle of iron railings. Keep to the path nearest to this tree to a cross path, the path to the right leading to this tree. Take the left hand path through some gorse bushes and when this path meets a cross path, turn left and continue descending over a number of main paths along roughly the same contour. The valley is on the right and on the opposite side there is a scar of the top of a quarry; this should be kept roughly 200 yards away as the descent ahead is gradually made towards a wooded hollow. The path goes through a disused quarry and descends steeply to the circular wood seen ahead.

Go over the fence into the wood and continue along a fence which is on the right. Make for a low iron-roofed barn. Turn right through a gate between a high wall and another barn. Follow the wall and go through a bridle gate following the path with the wall on the left. Cross a stile adjacent to a gate, go over a track, (with Postlip Hall on the left) into the spinney opposite via another stile with a footpath sign to

Winchcombe. Follow the path with a fence on the right. Pass over a stile and pass to the left of a barn and go over another stile. Continue along the edge of the field with a hedge on the left. At the end of the field go through this hedge and cross the concrete slab over the tiny stream. Turn right along a track with the stream now on the right to the mill.

At a car park for the paper mill, bear left (leaving the mill fire station on the right) and ascend to a T-junction. Here turn right and enter the mill yard again. (This seems somewhat circuitous but it follows the right of way). Continue straight ahead for 300 yards to pass through a kissing gate. In a further 150 yards the road bears left. Here go straight ahead over a stile and follow the fence on the right. Walk through three fields emerging on to the road on the outskirts of Winchcombe.

Ramble 7
DEADMANBURY GATE, LYNES BARN, PINNOCK, GUITING POWER

This is an excellent walk of the central portion of the North Cotswolds.
Map O.S. 163 in the 1/50000 series.
Starting point: Grid reference 057262 near Deadmanbury Gate.
Distance 10½ miles.

The starting point will probably be approached from Winchcombe. In this case take the road to the right of the George Hotel. Go along this road to the top of the hill and a little beyond at the fork bear left (signposted Guiting Power). In a further ¼ mile the entrance to Farmcote Wood Farm will be seen on the left (not signed). Continue for a further ¼ mile to a rough parking place on the right.

This is the start of the walk.

Walk back along the road just traversed towards Winchcombe for 100 yards to a track on the right with a bridleway sign. Follow the path and go ahead as it continues with a hedge immediately on the right to the cottages directly ahead. Pass to the right of these cottages into another field and go straight ahead on the left of the field and descend with a wood on the left to the road (Lynes Barn). Turn left and in 200 yards at the road junction turn right.

Go along this road, passing the road to Farmcote on the left, for ¾ mile. Take an overgrown sunken track (this is not easy to find) on the right which leads to Pinnock. Go straight ahead over the farm drive for ¾ mile along a rough lane. At the junction of this lane with a road turn

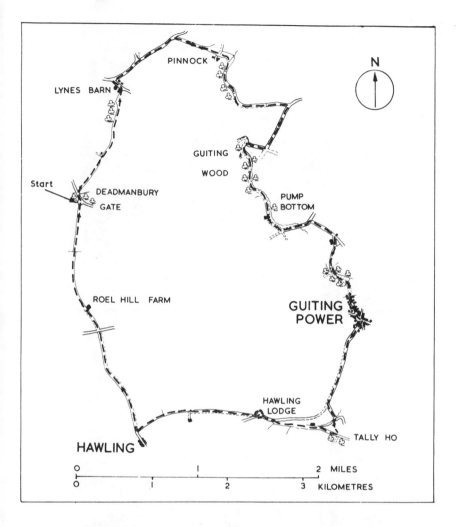

right. In less than ½ mile at the cross roads turn right and then at the junction turn sharp left. In just over ¾ mile, at the road junction, turn left. In ¼ mile take the farm road on the right to Castlett Farm (now called a Stud). Pass through the main farm entrance on the right and continue with the bulk of the farm on the right to the end of the farm house wall. Turn right to follow a wooden fence which is on the left to go through a bridle gate. Now keep to the fence on the right to a gate in the corner. Descend through the wood and cross the stream by the stone bridge. Turn left and follow the track to a road and then continue ahead into Guiting Power, a pleasant village. (5¾ miles have now been walked). There is a nature reserve which may be visited with permission. The church has two fine Norman doorways.

27

Guiting Power

But to continue the walk; turn opposite the bus shelter along a road which leads to the church. At the school, before reaching the church, turn right. In ¾ mile take a road on the left and follow it down for 200 yards to a point where there are three gates on the right. Go through the third gate i.e. the one straight ahead.

Cross the stream and follow the track to the left, passing close to a pond, to arrive at a farm road. Cross the road and immediately turn right into a field. Walk with a wall and the farm road on the right. Continue in the same direction to the road at Hawling Lodge.

Go straight ahead along the road through the farm buildings. At the last farm building on the right, where the road bends, take the ascending track on the right. Where the open track is followed by a hedge and wall continue in the same direction with this hedge and wall on the right over a number of stiles.

At the end of the wall, where there is a farm on the left, pass to the right of a new barn and go ahead in the same direction with a fence on the left. Pass into the next field and follow in the same direction with a wall on the left to a rough cartway.

Turn right and continue over several fields with a wall or hedge on the left for nearly a mile to the road. Cross the road and continue along Campden Lane, now well defined, past Roel Hill Farm, for ¾ mile to the road and the start and completion of the ramble.

Ramble 8
BLOCKLEY—BROAD CAMPDEN

This walk follows a circuitous anti-clockwise route with Northwick Park as the hub.
Map O.S. 151 in the 1/50000 series.
Starting point: Grid reference 165350 Blockley Parish Church.
Distance 10¾ miles.

Start at the church gate by the Royal British Legion building. Enter the churchyard taking the left hand path with the church to the right and down the path to the road. Turn right to go past the Lower Brook Hotel and take the first turn left after crossing the brook. Follow the road which merges into a farm track and, in about ¼ mile swings left towards Pasture Farm, but at this point leave the track to pass to the right of a modern barn. Go ahead up the field keeping close to the hedge on the right. Pass through the bridle gate and continue ahead to a line of trees at the top of the field; turn left. Follow the fence and hedge which merges into a stone wall. Continue with the wall on the right, cross over a stile and then through a gate into a small compound. About 30 yards on and to the left is a way-marked gate.

Pass through this gate and walk ahead, down the field, aiming for the right hand side of a short line of trees. There is a post with a way-mark at this point where the path drops over the remains of an old wall. Go downhill with the fence on the left to a gate about 100 yards ahead. Continue ahead, ignoring the next gate on the left (way-marked) in 50 yards, keep the wire fence on the left, cross a stile and pass by another gate. The path bears right and then left around a small plantation and through a gate towards a farm-house. Turn right in front of the house and go via the stile or wicket gate into a track by the side of the house on to the farm drive and continue down to the road.

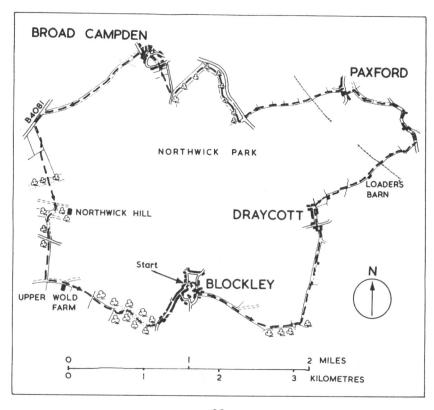

Walk down the road and go over the cross roads into Draycott. Continue down the village street until it turns left at the farmhouse facing you. At this point go through the field gate on the right and cross the field to a group of barns. To the left of these barns the right of way appears to be with the fence to the left but it proved impossible to do this. A gap on the left made the path appear to continue with the hedge on the right. This path crosses over a brook to a bridleway; turn left and go under the railway bridge and follow the hedge on the right to the road. Turn left and in about 250 yards the road passes through the group of cottages which have been visible on the left for some time. The road crosses a stream and, in about ¼ mile and after a sharp left turn, the roofs of the village of Paxford come into sight on the left. From this sharp left turn continue for 200 yards and then leave the road and go through a farm gate on the left and walk towards Paxford keeping the hedge on the left.

A gate leads on to a wider track with some houses across the field on the left. Look out for a stile on the left which will lead directly to the right hand end of a red brick wall at the end of the houses, and a second stile brings you into the road. Cross the road. Turn right towards Paxford and, in 200 yards, turn left off the road on to a track which crosses the brook by an iron-railed bridge and passes through farm buildings. The brook is now on the left and the path follows this towards the railway line visible ahead. Cross over the railway and continue to follow beside the brook across five fields to the road.

Turn left for about 10 yards, cross the road into the grounds of the Northwick Business Centre and immediately turn right into the wood and follow the path which is parallel to the road. (If the path is heavily overgrown and difficult to follow it may be better to stay on the road for this section of about 300 yards to a point where you can enter by a track and, turning right, get back to the woodland path of the main narrative.) The path through the wood crosses two farm tracks at right-angles and, shortly after the second one the path swings round to the left away from the road and continues for about 650 yards with Broad Campden becoming visible on the right. The path gets quite close to the road and a footpath on the right leads to it by a way-marked stile.

Across the road a stile with a footpath sign continues the route. Go over the stile and turn right and go down the meadow to pass through a wide gap in the hedge; continue the descent in the same direction. A stile leads to a narrow passage between the houses to the road. Across the road, the path is between two hedges with a tiny stream on the left. A bridge and the path lead into Broad Campden. At the road turn left, pass in front of the church and go ahead to the main road and the Baker's Arms Inn (6 miles have now been walked).

A few yards beyond the car park of the Baker's Arms there is a gate on the opposite side of the road with a bridleway signpost. Follow the bridleway for 1 mile to the road B4081 and here turn left. In 200 yards leave the road and take the signposted bridleway on the left for about 400 yards with the wall on the right. A gap in the wall leads into the adjacent field; continue in the same direction with the wall on the left. Make for the wood ahead to arrive at a point about 100 yards from the left corner of the field. Here a wicket gate into the strip of wood takes the path across a wide track to a gate on the opposite side.

Follow the wall which is on the right for 300 yards to join the drive to Northwick Hill Farm. Continue ahead into the valley bottom. Cross the intersecting tracks and continue ahead on the ascending track.

Cross a road and go down the track opposite. In 500 yards a drive to Upton Wold Farm is reached. Turn left. Go through the farm gate alongside the farm buildings, through a gap in a low hedge and by the garden wall. Continue ahead and pass through a gate into a field. Go ahead to the facing wood and enter it by a gate. Turn right and follow this track to the road in Blockley. Turn left and go ahead to the beginning of the walk.

Broad Campden

Ramble 9
KILKENNY, LINEOVER WOOD, CHATCOMBE WOOD, UPPER COBERLEY, COCKLEFORD, COWLEY, COBERLEY.

This is a good walk with some extensive views, remote rural hamlets and polished estates.

Map O.S. 163 in the 1/50000 series.

Starting point: Grid reference 004186 near Kilkenny, 4 miles south east of Cheltenham and 1½ miles south west of Andoversford.

Distance 10¾ miles.

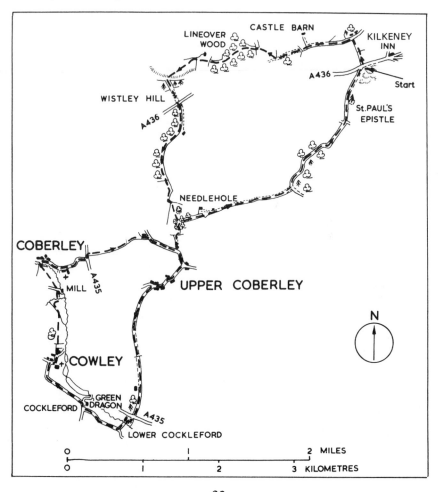

The start of the walk is on A436, 400 yards up the hill to the west of Kilkeney Inn which is in the hamlet of Kilkenny, although spelt differently.

At the starting point there is a minor road signposted Hilcot. Opposite this road go through a gate and cross two fields with a boundary hedge on the left. At this point there are fine views of the Malverns. Pass through a gateway to a metalled service road. Turn left. In 650 yards the road turns to the right to go to Castle Barn, but at this point leave the road and proceed straight on through the gateway, cross a field with a wall on the left and pass through a second gateway keeping a wire fence on the right.

At a pair of gates at the beginning of a wood, take the one on the right and follow a diagonal footpath down the hill with a wood on the left. At a gateway with a Cotswold Way sign, pass into Lineover Wood. Follow the track through the Wood. At a fork bear right (Cotswold Way sign), keeping an open field on the right. At the far edge of the wood pass through a small gate. Ascend the hill pasture, with a farmhouse and buildings about 100 yards to the right, in the direction of a rough coppice so as to reach it about 50 yards below some scree on the steep hillside on the left.

At the coppice, pass through a gap in the scrub to a gate just to the left. Pass through this gate and follow a narrow path keeping a mixed coppice with a wire fence on the right.

Just before the coppice swings to the right, take a diagonal path—little more than a sheep track—to rise across the face of the hill to arrive at a bridleway on the plateau topping the hill. Cross this bridleway and go through a gateway with a sheepfold to the right. Continue through a small covert and in the same direction to A436.

Cross straight over to a bridleway running along just inside Chatcombe Wood. Look out for deer. Follow this bridleway alongside a wood for 3/4 mile to a gate. Through the gate make for the hedge on the left and to the two pylons in front. Just before the pylons go through the bridle gate. From here walk across the field in front diagonally so as to bear away from the hedge on the right, passing under two lots of power lines to the right in midfield, of a small hollow covered with scrub trees, to arrive at the right hand edge of the coppice in front. Enter the coppice and in a few yards follow the bridle track to the right.

On leaving the coppice continue along the bridleway with a hedge on the left. Go through a gate and continue along a bridleway with the hedge now on the right, to the road with a signpost Wistley Hill. Turn left and in 200 yards turn right and walk to Upper Coberley. Pass through the gateway of Lower Farm at the end of the hamlet. Immediately through this gateway, turn left up the rough bridleway and follow it without deviation. Continue past a large barn on the right. The bridleway now becomes a metalled one. Just before the main road, the wood on the right is called Tomtits Bottom.

The main road is A435. Cross this and go down the track opposite, to pass in front of a house in a charming setting, to a bridge. Cross the River Churn by this stone bridge. Go up the path and at the subsidiary road turn right. At the T-junction turn right and in about 100 yards, opposite the Green Dragon Inn at Cockeleford, turn left.

Walk along the road with Cowley Manor on the right. At the T-junction turn right and bear left at the entrance gates of the Manor. Continue along the road until it bends to the right to go downhill. At this point, where there is a notice "Churnside Camp and Adventure Centre", take a track on the left which has some buildings on the right. In 50 yards go over a stile into a field with a hedge and wall on the left. At the end of the wall go over the facing fence and walk to the right of a small coppice and continue in the same direction to a hedge. Go through a gap in this hedge and then follow the well defined path alongside this same hedge which is now on the left. In about 50 yards a facing hedge is reached. Turn right and still following a well defined path go for about 85 yards. Turn through the hedge on the left to follow a path descending to a bridge.

From the bridge ascend the other bank to a field. Cross this field, with a house away on the right, to a fence. Walk with this fence on the right to a gate with a footpath sign on the other side of it. Cross the green lane to a stile on the opposite side which also has a footpath sign. Enter the field and then make for the village of Coberley seen in the distance. In a short distance a path becomes obvious. At the corner of the field go over a stile, cross the stone bridge and follow the slope up to a kissing gate on the road at Coberley. Turn right. Follow the road round right towards the church. At some dignified buildings on the right, there is a way through an archway to the church and it is worth while to go this way to see the charming gardens with the church just beyond. Continue past these buildings for about 300 yards and at the main road, cross with care and turn left.

In about 25 yards go up the bank on the right to a wicket gate. Continue up the next field with a hedge and fence on the right for 700 yards. At the top of this field go through a gate and continue ascending with the hedge and fence still on the right. Go through a gate preceding some buildings; continue along a definite track through a gate to the road. At this subsidiary road turn right and in ¼ mile there is the signpost on the left which says Wistley Hill.

Here turn left and follow the hedge on the left. At the top of the field go through the gateway and continue in the same direction, with a hedge now on the right, to a coppice. Continue along a track through the coppice to a gate and rise to the farm road with the house, Needlehole, on the left. Turn right and go along this pleasant track, with good views, to the T-junction. Turn left and go along this road to A436 and the beginning of the ramble.

Ramble 10
BEMBOROUGH, EYFORD PARK, NAUNTON, BARTON, GUITING POWER, KINETON

A walk of rolling downs and interesting villages.
Map O.S. 163 in the 1/50000 series.
Starting point: Grid reference 107272 at a lane leading to Bemborough Farm.
Distance 11½ miles.

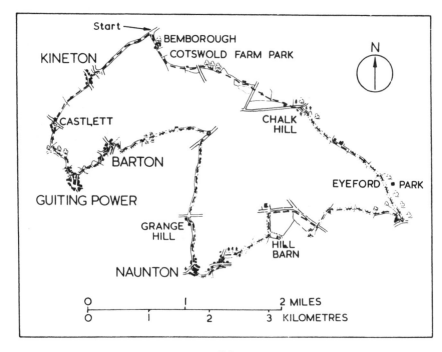

To get to the starting point take the Snowshill road from Broadway. On entering Snowshill bear left to leave the church on the right. Continue over two minor cross roads to the T-junction which is ¾ mile from Snowshill. Turn right and in 2½ miles cross the B4077 road. Continue for a further mile and then take a lane on the right signposted Kineton. In ¼ mile take the lane on the left to Bemborough Farm.

Bemborough Farm devotes one section of about 50 acres to the preservation of some domestic animals which are threatened with extinction because their continuance has ceased to be economic. It is a most interesting enterprise and visitors may go round this part of the farm from April to September on payment of a small entrance fee.

Walk into the farmyard then turn right and go through a gate. Follow the track through four fields and go over the stile into the road. Turn left, and in a few yards turn right down an overgrown track, with a thicket on the left and a hedge on the right. At the edge of the thicket the track turns left, following the thicket. Do not follow it but go through a gateway straight ahead and continue SE in the same direction as before, passing just to the left of a quarry. At the junction with a subsidiary road, cross the wall opposite. (If farming operations make this difficult then to get to the "Private" road which leads into Eyford Park take this simpler way. On coming to the subsidiary road turn right. At the T-junction turn left and continue until the "Private" road is reached). Go straight ahead across the field to the far right-hand corner. Follow the hedge on the right in the next field towards Chalk Hill Farm. Pass just to the left of the farm buildings and cross the wall almost in the corner of the field beyond the farm, near to a pond, into a road. Turn left and in about 200 yards take a road to the right marked "Private" which leads through Eyford Park. This continues for 1¾ miles, becoming a grass track for a time.

At the main road turn right, and immediately right again, and walk along the track with some cottages on the left. Continue straight ahead through a gate. Follow the ascending track keeping to a wall on the left. Where the wall ends pass through a gate in the facing wall and continue in the same direction along a definite track through two fields to a barn. Turn left along a track to the road. Cross this with care and just beyond the gate opposite turn right to follow the wall on the right for ½ mile. On reaching a track turn left along it, away from the road. When the track turns left to Hill Barn keep straight ahead down into a hollow and then turn right. In a few yards cross a small stream and follow the unploughed path over the hill into a coppice. Through the coppice go along a good track into Naunton. (6 miles have now been walked.)

At the main road in the village turn left, and just before the Black Horse Inn, turn right, cross the stream, the Windrush, turn right and walk with the stream on the right. When a track comes in from the right, continue straight ahead to the road. Turn right, go over the river bridge and take the first road on the left. Follow this uphill for ½ mile to Grange Hill Farm at the subsidiary road. Cross the road and continue northwards up a good track for ¾ of a mile to the road. Turn right, and in 250 yards take the cart road on the left. Follow this over four fields and go over a fence into a narrow passage which descends to the left into Barton. Turn right along the road and take the first track on the left between some buildings on the right and a pond on the left. Continue past a track on the right which leads to Castlett Farm. Go between the farm buildings ahead, and pass over three stiles. Bear right, making for the left corner of a facing hedge running to the right. Continue in the same direction with a hedge on the right. Cross a stone stile in this hedge, turn left and go downhill over a stream and then upwards to a wooden stile. Here do not cross the stile, but turn right, and bear round to the left and up a path past a cottage to a lane. Turn right along the lane, and go through a gate and down a track to a stream. Go over the stone bridge on the right and up a path on the other side to a gate. Cross the field to Castlett Farm. Pass between the buildings to a cottage in front. Go through a gate on the left of the cottage, cross a stile in the corner behind the cottage, and go up the next field with a hedge on the right. Bear left into the next field, and walk with a hedge on the right over two fields to the road at Kineton. Turn left and continue through the village to the Half Way House pub. Take the track immediately to the left of the pub. This leads to a garden but the right of way is on the right of the garden. Go downhill to a stone bridge. Cross this and then turn right up the road to the beginning of the walk.

Ramble 11
MICKLETON, HIDCOTE BOYCE, ILMINGTON, HIDCOTE BARTRIM.

A varied walk taking in the pleasant places of Ebrington,
Foxcote, Hidcote Boyce and Hidcote Bartrim.
Map O.S. 151 in the 1/50000 series.
Starting point: Grid reference 161435 Village of Mickleton.
Distance 11½ miles.

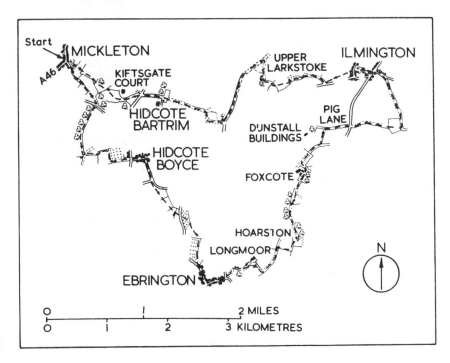

From the A46, take the lane to Mickleton Church. Pass the church car park, bear left and in 10 yards, turn right up a grassy bank to a wicket gate into a field. Cross the field, keeping close to the hedge on the right and in 100 yards drop down to a gate and cross the brook, then walk along a path through trees to a wicket gate. Go through the next field keeping near to the hedge on the left, to another wicket gate. Turn right and go to the top left hand corner and so to the road.

Cross the road and climb the bank. Go through a gate, turn right and follow the edge of the field with a wood on the right. In about 200 yards go through a wicket gate into the wood. Go along a path through the wood near a fence on the left. On coming out of the wood, continue in

39

the same direction to a black barn and the entrance to Starveal Farm. Turn left at the barn and go straight across the farm road to follow the hedge which is on the left. Continue to and cross the brook by the footbridge into the next field. Turn sharp left and follow the hedge which is on the left. Continue to follow it round the field as it turns to the right up the field. At the top of the field, where there is an electricity pole go into the cart track on the left. Follow this to the road. Go up the road opposite to Hidcote Boyce.

Turn right at the top of the village and follow the road for ¼ mile to a right turn, signposted Ebrington. Take the right lane and in 5 yards go through a gate on the left. Walk with the hedge on the left. Where the hedge bears left, keep the same direction, crossing the next hedge. Then go through a gap in the next hedge. Pass to the right of the barn immediately ahead and through a gate. Continue up the slope to a gate giving access to the road. Go straight over the road and through the gate opposite into an orchard and pass through this orchard keeping the same direction to a fence. Over the fence bear right and drop down to the left hand corner of the orchard ahead (South East). Pass over a stile and continue through the orchard with a hedge on the left to a track and so to the road. (3 miles have now been walked).

Turn left into Ebrington (locally known as Yubberton). Follow the Charington road through the village. About 150 yards past the end of the village, at the top of an ascent, there is a road on the left with a 'No through road' sign. Immediately beyond this there is a farm road on the left marked Longmoor. Take this road and at the pillar entrance to Longmoor Farm follow the fence which is on the left.

At the end of the fence where the track makes a T-junction with another track turn right. In about 200 yards follow the track round to the left and walk with a hedge on the right. At the end of this field, i.e. about 500 yards from the left turn already referred to, and where the track peters out and where a hedge runs up on the left, turn right at a large ash tree alongside an old shed. Descend to the facing hedge; there is a brook just beyond the hedge.

Turn left and in just over 100 yards go through a gap on the right and over a brook. Immediately turn left and in 30 yards go through a gate. Turn sharp right and follow the hedge which is on the right to a farm track. Turn left and pass to the right of the Hoarston Farm buildings. Go for 100 yards past the last building and at a large electricity pylon veer left towards the trees beyond which there is the brook in the valley. Follow these trees and hedge to the right to a gate through which there is an old farm building. Go ahead along the contour of the hill walking parallel to the hedge on the left. In a little while the charming Foxcote House can be seen through the trees across the valley. Continue to a gate in the wood ahead. After 100 yards where the track curves left to the outbuildings of Foxcote, keep straight ahead to the right of a small stream for 50 yards. Cross a fence on to a track coming down from the right and turn left to rise up to the park road. (5 miles have now been walked.)

Turn right and after passing a stone barn high up on the left called Dunstall Buildings, turn left into the field and ascend with a hedge on the right. At the top of the ascent enter a bridleway (Pig Lane); turn right. Go over a road (but if desired to go direct to Ilmington go left) and continue on the bridleway to the bottom of the hill. Turn left into Ilmington. (7½ miles have now been walked). Refreshments are available at the Red Lion Inn.

Leaving the Inn, turn right uphill and in 100 yards right again at a house with a bay window. Follow the footpath to the Church and pass along two sides of the churchyard. At the road, turn left. In 50 yards, turn right and continue in the same direction up a track leading through a gate into a field. Walk to the top and in a further 100 yards (do not descend to the road on the left which is only 15 yards away), turn right along a cart track.

Follow the cart track but where it turns right towards a barn go over the stile straight ahead along a track between wooden fences. After coming out of this track continue ahead following a fence which is on the left and descend to a stile and gate. Over the stile go straight ahead ascending the field making for a point about 100 yards to the left of a prominent tree on the top of the ascent. Descend in the same direction to a bridge which crosses a ditch. Across the bridge bear right to a signposted kissing gate. Cross the tiny brook, pass through the thicket, and ascend the field. About 100 yards to the left of Upper Larkstoke Farm go through a signposted gate and ascend the path through the young plantation. At a T-junction with another path turn right as indicated by a waymark. Cross a ditch into the next field. Veer slightly left (compass bearing 340°), ascend and make for the right hand side of some brushwood which is to the right of a prominent tree on the field boundary. At the road turn left uphill to the radio station. Take the good track to the right which leads to the National Trust car park at Hidcote Manor.

Continue ahead to the T-junction, then cross to the signpost and go through the nearby gate in the wall. This gives access to parkland to the left of Kiftsgate Court. Go down into the valley keeping to the right of a stream. Pass through several gates. On entering the field next to the church, bear slightly right round the new cemetery and so down the lane into Mickleton.

Ramble 12
ELMLEY CASTLE AND KEMERTON

A ramble round Bredon

Map O.S. 150 in the 1/50000 series.

Starting point: Grid reference 982411 Village of Elmley Castle.

Distance 12 miles.

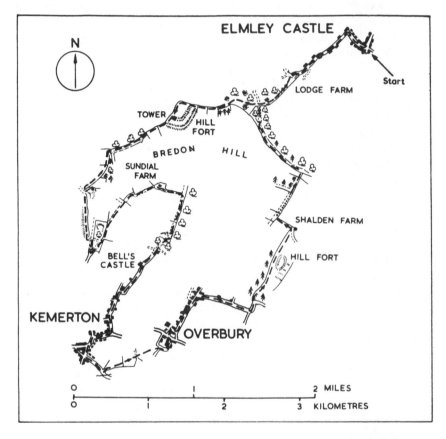

Proceeding up the main street of Elmley Castle turn right immediately past the Queen Elizabeth Inn. Follow the road for ¾ mile and at the entrance to Lodge Farm on the left continue ahead up the sunken track. Fifty yards past a gate, where 5 tracks meet, bear left up a faint grass track which can just be seen winding its way up the hill. Keep to the track, bearing left to a fence on the left and walk uphill and parallel to the fence. Go ahead through a gate to the next field and follow the fence uphill, crossing the track coming down through a gate on the left. Do not go through the gate. Continue ahead for 50 yards and just round the corner of the wood bear right up a narrow path. In a few yards go along the side of the hill, gradually rising to a wire fence at the top. Keep ahead to a gate next to a wood on the left.

Pershore can be seen across the valley 3½ miles away. Continue with the wall on the right to the tower on the summit. Follow the path to the right of the tower, alongside the wall on the right, to the second gate and walk through a coppice. Now walk along a track with a narrow belt of trees on the right for ¼ mile. When the track and fence on the left turn left bear right on a narrow path for 20 yards and pass through a bridle gate. After passing through the bridle gate turn sharp left and follow the wall which is on the left for over ⅓ mile. Follow the wall round and continue along a definite track with a fence on the left and a valley on the right for ⅓ mile to the end of the fence. Turn left and in 50 yards turn right along a definite track. Go through a gate and descend to a very rough road. Here turn sharp left and walk uphill. When the track turns sharp left continue ahead between hedges to a gate and stile. In the field beyond keep alongside the fence on the left for 100 yards and then bear right to follow a hedge on the left, which runs up between two fields in an intermittent way without forming a definite barrier. Go through the gate ahead to follow the track to Sundial Farm. The farm house has been demolished, but the face of the sundial can be seen on the gable end of the barn facing south. Follow the track round the barn, keeping the buildings on the left, until the track makes a T-junction with another track. Here turn right to descend with a wall on the left. As the track meets a field gate and a side gate, by some old quarry workings, go through the side gate, down past some farm buildings on the left to a metalled road. Follow the road down the hill, passing Bell's Castle, which is on the right, into Kemerton (6½ miles have now been walked).

At the War Memorial preceding the Crown Inn, bear left down the lane and then take the first turn on the left down a minor lane, which merges into a bridle road. At the stream, instead of going down the bridleway ahead, turn left and go through a gate into a field and bear right, ENE, across a marshy field with no defined track. Go through a gate in the middle of the hedge between two willows to next field, keep ENE to a cart track. Cross this and go over a fence, a stream, and another fence to the next field, and keep in the same direction towards the gate in front of the farm buildings seen in the distance.

Cross the farm road and follow the track to the right of the farm buildings and then bear left to the main road. Turn left then right to go past Overbury Church. Turn right at Overbury Hall, then in a few yards left, and ascend through the village. At the fork (ahead the sign-post indicates no through road), turn right. Follow this road, ignoring the first cart track on the left, and, where the road turns sharp right downhill, take the left hand cart track uphill. Then in a few yards bear left at the fork and ascend with a conifer wood on the left. In a short distance go through a gate into an open field and follow the track with a wall on the left.

At Shalden Farm (now a ruin), go sharp left and through a field with a wall on the right. *Go through the next gate and turn right up a bridleway. Continue straight ahead through gates*, past conifers on the left, to a path turning along the edge of Bredon. Turn left and follow the edge with a wood on the right. Pass through the next gate and continue along the edge with a fence and a wood on the right. In less than ½ mile there is a gate on the right and this leads into a track which runs between woods. Go down this track and through the gate at the bottom. Immediately through the gate turn right. This is the same path which was taken at the beginning of the walk. Descend now along the track into Elmley Castle.

*The part in italics is not a right of way but the Overbury Estate will not object to a limited use provided it is understood that there is no acceptance of a right of way.

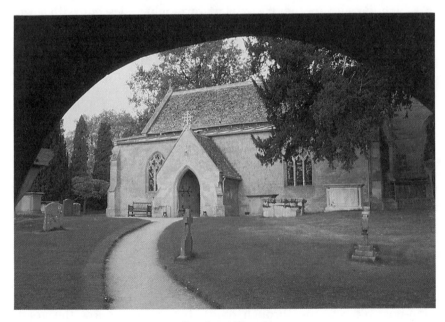

Overbury Church

Ramble 13
STUMPS CROSS, LYNES BARN, PUMP BOTTOM, GUITING POWER, TEMPLE GUITING.

Guiting Woods and Campden Lane make this a favourite ramble.
Maps O.S. 150 and 163. in the 1/50000 series.
Starting point: Grid reference 076303 Stumps Cross.
Distance 12 miles.

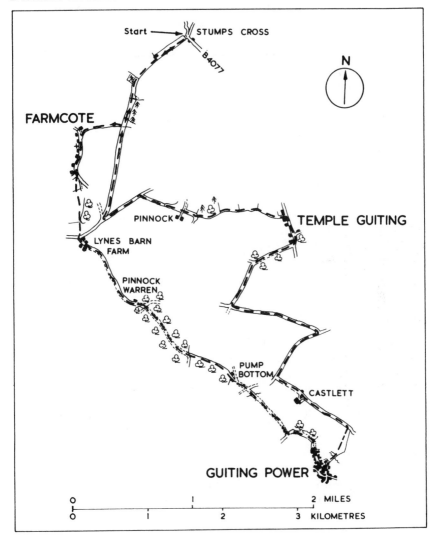

Start near Stanway at 076303 Stumps Cross on B4077 at the top of Stanway Hill (note the actual stump). From the road pass through a gate into a cart track Campden Lane which is signposted 'Farmcote 2.5 km'. Go along this track through two more gateways when the track soon becomes a broad bridleway. After going through the second gate, and just past the wood on the right, Beckbury Camp may be seen on the right. Just before the third gateway the track forks. Take the right hand fork and go through the gateway. The track now descends. From the bottom of the descent go a further 60 yards and turn right along an overgrown cart track with a wall on the left, and descend into the village of Farmcote. At the road turn left past some distinguished houses and the tiny St. Faith's Chapel.

At the end of the main part of the village continue ahead to go past a house called The Cottage. The house may not have any sign, but it is at a point where there is a green triangle of land in front, and an entrance on the right into some farm buildings. There is a cattle grid in the entrance and a box for mail. A few yards further on there is a gate on the right. The right of way is over the wall 10 yards past this gate. Until this difficult obstruction is removed, go through the gate.

Follow the poplars which are on the left. At the last poplar turn left through the gap and make for the small iron gate. After passing through this gate continue in the same direction to go through another gate.

Go ahead in the same general direction making towards the left hand corner of the field, so as to arrive at the facing hedge at a gate which is about 30 yards from the wood on the left.

From this gate ascend to the buildings on the skyline and go to the road. Turn left, and then go down the road on the right which has a notice 'Not suitable for motor vehicles'.

In ¾ mile the cottage of Pinnock Warren with a channelled stream in front is reached. In about 200 yards past this cottage, where the road turns left, there are two waymarked tracks on the right. Take the left hand one uphill and go for nearly ¾ mile without deviation to where the wood on the left finishes, and the track turns sharp right. Do not turn right but go straight ahead down an overgrown path with an open field on the left and a wood on the right. This track goes over a stile and continues to the right of a cottage to the road at Pump Bottom. Turn right, and in 250 yards continue over the road to go along the rough cartway. In ½ mile, at a farm road which runs uphill to the right, turn left and immediately on the left, take a green path down through a thicket to a stream. Continue ahead, with the stream on the left, to ascend to a road which leads into Guiting Power. Turn left to the Green. (5 miles have now been walked).

Turn left down the lane at the end of the Green opposite the War

Memorial. This is a cul-de-sac and leads to a tiny brook. Pass over the brook and then go over the stile to the left of a gate. Descend with the brook now on the right to a bridge over a stream. Ascend to two stiles and go over the one in front. Cross the field, keeping the hedge on the right about 50 yards away, to a wall. Go over the stile into the road and turn left. Leaving Castlett Farm on the left and a cottage on the right, go down the farm lane to a road. At the road turn right and in ½ mile take the rough lane on the left. In ¾ mile take the first turn on the right. Walk straight ahead for ¾ mile to the road at Temple Guiting. Turn left and in ¼ mile, between two cottages on the left, go up the fenced-in green track on the left. Go through a bridle gate and continue up a fenced track to another bridle gate. Go over three fields with a wall or fence on the left to a wood. Follow through the wood to the stream at Pinnock. Across the stream go up the road to the right. In 200 yards cross a farm road and go through the gate opposite. Continue ahead and pass over a stile into a coppice and follow the sunken track to a metalled road. Turn left and in less than ½ mile turn right and immediately take a track on the right.

Now continue along this bridle track for 1½ miles to the beginning of the walk at Stumps Cross.

Ramble 14
HAZLETON, ASTON BLANK

This ramble is in delightfully remote rolling country and takes in the villages of Hazleton, Notgrove, Aston Blank and Turkdean.
Map. O.S. 163 in the 1/50000 series.
Starting point: Grid reference 076172 Puesdown Inn on A40(T) between Andoversford and Northleach.
Distance 12 miles.

Face the Puesdown Inn and go into the Inn Yard to the left of the Inn, and over a stile in the extreme left hand corner, ignoring any obstructions. Walk through one field with the wall on the left, a distance of about 500 yards. At a rough lane, turn left and walk ½ mile to the village of Hazleton. At the point where the rough lane makes a T-junction with a subsidiary road, turn right, and in 30 yards, turn left, and in another 80 yards turn left again at the T-junction.

Continue along the lane until the church is seen on the right. Immediately beyond the church continue over a lane into a good farm track. On passing to the left of the farm go over two fields with a wall on the right.

Pass through a gate and follow a wall which is on the left over another two fields to an avenue of trees with a wall on each side. At the end of this avenue, where there is an entrance to Salperton Park on the left, turn right. Walk along this good farm track for a mile to Farhill Farm. Here this farm track merges into an indefinite grass track slightly to the right. Descend with a wall on the left which ends in a few yards. Continue descending in the same direction for a ¼ mile to a gate at the bottom of the descent.

Through this turn right and in 200 yards at a fence turn left uphill. In 250 yards pass through a gate in a wire fence. Continue ahead for a further 200 yards in the same direction, and pass through a gate into a good farm track. Pass to the right of Kitehill Barn and go on to the road. Immediately in front are the attractive metal gates of Notgrove Manor with the design of a mermaid with two tails.

Turn left and in 200 yards turn right towards the village of Notgrove. The village with its gracious manor house is most attractive. The church has a Saxon survival on the outside east wall, some very fine Norman arches and a beautiful modern tapestry.

At the crossroads (a sort of walled circle) at the beginning of the village, turn left downhill for about 250 yards. Turn into the first lane on the right, and in another 250 yards where the lane bears right, go through the gate in front. Walk diagonally to the left, towards the wood, with a gate to the left of it. Beyond the gate is a rough lane, turn right, and after about 75 yards pass through a gate straight ahead, and immediately turn left up the field with a charming avenue of trees on the left. In 70 yards pass through a gate and continue ahead with the

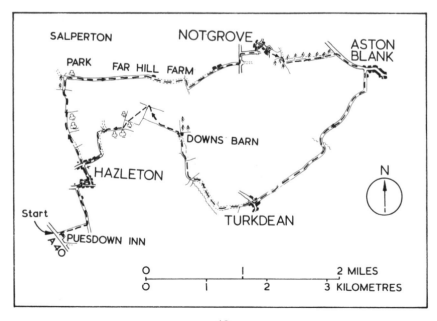

wood still on the left. At the end of this field pass into the avenue of trees and continue to the road. Turn right and walk to Aston Blank. (Aston Blank has the alternative name of Cold Aston; Blank and Cold having the same meaning). The Plough Inn is towards the end of the village. (5½ miles have now been walked).

From the Plough Inn, go back westward, along the road previously traversed, continue past the church, and in about 150 yards turn left down a cart track, and follow it for 2 miles to Turkdean. At the Turkdean T-junction turn right, and in a few yards left down a rough lane, which after a few yards arrives at a gate. Continue along this track which gradually deteriorates.

In roughly ¾ mile before a gate the track forks. On the left, through a gate, the track leads directly to Hazleton and this is the shorter and may be followed. The more interesting way is through the gate straight ahead and this is the one now described.

Continue along the valley bottom, with its satisfying contours, for ¾ mile. Go through the first gate on the left at a point where there is a crossing of the tiny stream. Follow the track through the rough pasture rising gradually to Downs Barn which is immediately to the left of the wood seen ahead.

From now on the narrative should be followed very carefully.

A few yards after passing the barn there is a wall on the left. At the wall turn left and walk so as to have the wall on the left. Continue for 350 yards to the top of a slight incline. At this point it is possible by looking diagonally to the right to see the corner of the field. Walk diagonally to the right to that corner, go over the wall and then immediately turn left through an iron gate. Walk down the field on a compass bearing of 235°, or if a compass is not available then walk down the field at an angle of 45° to the wall on the left. (If before the reference to taking a compass bearing there are obstructions, i.e. say a ploughed field or an electrified fence then an alternative is possible. Follow the wall which is on the left. At the end of this field turn right and follow the fence which is on the left and in 200 yards go through a gate on the left. Descend straight down and pass through the spinney.) Soon a spinney will appear in the valley below. Continue in the same direction making for the right hand side of the spinney, to a gate in the facing fence. Pass through the gate and immediately descend to and through the spinney to the definite track at the bottom of the valley. Turn right, go through the gateway and go along the definite track with a wood on the left. In about 500 yards follow the track uphill to the left. At the road continue to the church in the village of Hazleton.

Take the road on the left and at the next T-junction turn right. From here take the opposite way to that followed at the beginning of the walk.

Ramble 15
COLESBOURNE, WITHINGTON

A varied ramble of hills and woodland.
Map O.S. 163 in the 1/50000 series.
Starting point: Grid reference 999132 Colesbourne village.
Distance 12½ miles.

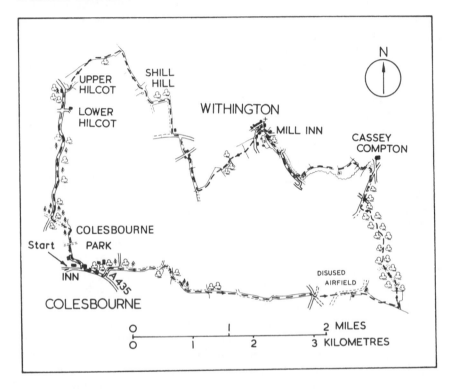

From the Colesbourne Inn walk along the main road (A435) towards Cirencester to the turning to Withington. Turn left and in 300 yards where the road turns sharp left leave the road to go straight ahead up the bridleway. Continue along the bridleway ignoring those tracks on each side which lead into fields until in ½ mile a definite fork in the track is reached: bear right and continue to, and go through, a field gate. Go ahead with a fence on the left for about 60 yards, then turn right along a raised bank and follow it to a gate and go through into a sunken track. Ascend this track, pass through a gate and continue to ascend with an open field on the left and trees and a fence on the right. At the end of the field go through a gate and continue ascending with a wall and plantation on the left. Continue to a metalled

50

farm road. Follow this for ½ mile and at the main cross roads take the road signposted "Chedworth".

Go along the road for 300 yards and then turn left on to a disused airfield ring road, signposted "Bridleway". Follow this round, passing a turning to some sheds on the right, to where it turns sharp left. Here go straight ahead through a gate. Follow the fence and wood on the right for 60 yards. Turn right and walk to a wall. Turn left and follow the wall over 2 fields to where there are two wicket gates in the corner. Just before the two wicket gates turn left and follow the wall. Pass over two stiles into a wood.

A few yards into the wood take the main path on the left. On reaching the cross-path (signposted 'Roman Villa' to the right) go straight ahead. Go along this path for ½ mile. At this point, at the bottom of a descent, there is a definite ascending track on the right. Avoid this and continue ahead to a metalled road. Turn right along the road over an old railway bridge and on up the hill. About 100 yards beyond the brow of the hill there is a wooden fence on the left. Go over the fence and follow a sunken grass track, bearing left at a fork halfway down to go round the hill above Cassey Compton.

At the far side drop down to and go through a gate. Follow the fence on the right and go over the stile. Cross the river by the footbridge. Follow the fence which is on the left and pass over a stile. Follow the hedge which is on the right and pass through the facing gate. Turn left and follow the hedge and fence which is on the left which leads to a stile. Go over the stile and continue in the same direction on the side of the hill. On coming to a hedge keep to the right of it for ¼ mile passing over a stone wall by a stile in the course of the ¼ mile. Pass to the right of a cottage and go through a gate on to a definite track. Turn right and in a few yards pass under an old railway bridge. At the T-junction turn right for 400 yards to where the road turns right. Here turn left and follow the path along the stream to go through the back of the Mill Restaurant buildings and so to the road in Withington. (6½ miles have now been walked).

From the Mill Inn go along the road over the river Coln and up the hill. Take the first turn on the left and in 100 yards turn left again. 80 yards from this turning where the road bears left go over the wooden fence on the right in the corner of the field. Go diagonally, ascending the field so as to arrive at a facing fence about 150 yards from the right boundary of the field. At the time of writing a passage through the barbed wire has been made. (If barbed wire continues to be a problem there is a gate on the right).

After passing through the barbed wire continue in roughly the same direction up the field towards a space between a wood on the left and a line of trees on the right WSW (compass bearing 251°). Pass under some electricity lines preceding this space to arrive at a gate. (That describes the right of way but a simpler way and one which the farmer would probably prefer would be as follows:

After leaving the road over the fence in the corner of the field, follow the fence which is on the right to a gate. Pass into the next field and continue with a fence on the right to a facing hedge. Turn left and walk with a hedge on the right for about 200 yards. Pass under some electricity lines and turn right up a gulley to a gate in a fence.)

Pass through the gate and follow the wood which is on the left to a large stone standing upright. Turn right, and pass through a gate in the fence on the left. Turn right and walk to the corner of the field. Turn left, and follow the hedge which is on the right for 500 yards to a farm track.

Turn right along this track for ¼ mile to the road. Cross the road and go along the track immediately opposite. Keep to the fence and hedge on the left across the field to another road. Turn left and in 150 yards pass an old iron barn. In a few yards past this, turn right. Follow this track for 500 yards to a gate which gives access to a wood. A few yards before this gate turn left and keep near the hedge on the left. Go through the gate straight ahead and immediately turn right along a hedge. In 250 yards pass a water hole which is on the left in some rough ground. Veer left to a field gate in the facing hedge. Go through and ascend a field with a wall on the right. At the end of a second field go through a gate and turn left and walk along the ridge with the valley on the left. Keeping to the fence on the left walk along the edge of the field, and in ½ mile just after passing under some power lines turn left to go through a gate. Descend gradually into the valley and on coming to the track at the bottom, turn right towards a black and white farmhouse which is Upper Hilcot Farm.

At the farm turn left and go along the road for 1¼ miles to where two stone pillars are set in a wall on the left. Turn in here and go along a bridleway for 400 yards to where it enters a field. Turn right and follow the edge of the field to some iron park gates on the right. Go through and immediately turn left through a field gate. Follow the edge of the field alongside some trees on the left to a lane. Follow this downhill over a stream and so up to Colesbourne.

Ramble 16
BOURTON DOWNS, HINCHWICK, FORD, CUTSDEAN, STANWAY ASH PLANTATION

An easy ramble mostly on the level but with pleasant undulations. It has a special richness of flora.
This walk is well worth while just for the lovely valley from Hornsleasow Quarry to Hinchwick.
Maps O.S. 150 & 151 in the 1/50000 series.
Starting point: Grid reference 130322: a disused quarry 2½ miles west of Bourton-on-the-Hill and 2 miles east south east of Snowshill.
Distance 12½ miles.

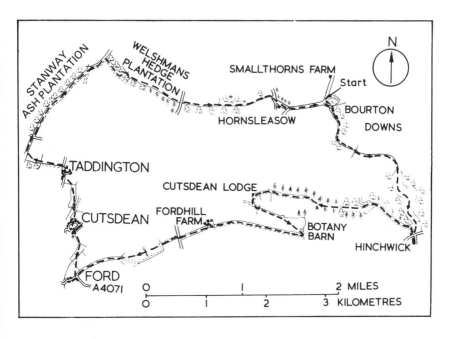

To reach the starting point from Broadway, take the A44 Oxford road up Fish Hill. Continue for 5 miles to where the A424 forks off to the right to Stow-on-the-Wold. Follow the A424 and in 200 yards take the road on the right (signposted Snowshill). In about 1 mile bear left up the hill (signposted Bourton-on-the-Water and Stow-on-the-Wold). In ½ mile just before the bottom of a descent, there is a quarry on the left. This is the start of the ramble.
Continue down the road; at the lowest point of the curve below the

53

quarry, turn left and follow the wall on the right eastwards along the bottom of the quarry.

Just beyond a detached concrete wall in the disused quarry at a fork bear right along a descending bridleway and go through a thicket. Crossing a bridleway which descends from the left, continue down the valley through a narrow wood with a wall on the right for 500 yards. At the end of the wood follow the wall for a further ¼ mile to where the boundaries of four fields meet. Turn right through a wicket gate into the adjoining field and then immediately turn left to continue down the enchanting valley for a little over a mile.

At the end of the wood on the right (with Hinchwick seen in front) pass through a gate. Bear right to a farm road. (Do not go into Hinchwick).

Turn right and walk with the wood on the right, following this road for ½ mile and at a sort of rough lay-by on the right and 100 yards before the road sweeps up to the right, leave the road to bear left down a green track into the valley bottom keeping to the edge of the wood which is on the right. In a few yards the path forks. Take the left hand one. Follow the track which passes into a coppice.

At a clearing there is a rough new made road running up to the right. Take the green track straight ahead which is the first to the left of the new road. The path rises and eventually comes to Custdean Lodge, a disused farmstead. Bear left and in 350 yards a well-defined track is reached.

Turn left. In 100 yards there are two gateways. Go through the right hand one. Continue with a wall on the left. In about 400 yards, where the wall begins to bear left and descends slightly, there is a gate on the left. Leave the wall to bear right across the field on a compass bearing of 130°. (If a compass is not available then bear right to make an angle of about 30° with the wall on the left). This leads to the ruins of an old barn, Botany Barn. (It may be that the ruins of Botany Barn will not immediately be found. If the walker gets to a wall and there is a farm road on the other side, it means a point has been reached to the right of Botany Barn. In that case, turn left along the wall to the ruins of Botany Barn. If, on the other hand, there is a field on the other side of the wall, it means that a point has been reached to the left of Botany Barn. In that case follow the wall to the right until the ruins of Botany Barn are seen.)

At the barn turn sharp right, along the far side of a wall which formed the boundary of the field just crossed. This track, which runs almost due west for 1 mile, leads to the buildings at Fordhill Farm.

Turn left down the farm road past the house and then turn right up the hill to the road. Cross the road, and a little to the right, take the track on the right of the wall. After 200 yards this track turns left, (the track is the easiest way but it is not the right of way) but continue straight ahead across a field to drop down through bushes into another field and on the left of a hedge to rejoin the track. Continue down to the Plough Inn at Ford. (7 miles have now been walked.)

Looking slightly to the left across the road from the Plough Inn, there is a wicket gate at the bend of the road. Go through. There may be no visible footpath but go straight ahead in the direction of Cutsdean village seen ahead. Pass through a broken wall and descend into a valley on the left. Drop down to a kissing gate through which a stream flows in wet weather. From here bear right up the hill to the diagonal corner to another kissing gate. Turn left along a hedge which is followed by a wall. Go past the church, which is on the left, to a gate leading to the road in Cutsdean.

A path goes across a walled paddock, round which the village is built, to cross another road and through the gate opposite. 20 yards ahead a gate leads to a field and straight ahead another gate leads to a farm track. Immediately after this gate turn left through a kissing gate. Go down and round the descent to a small gate. Cross the little River Windrush which rises ½ mile up the valley. Curving round the hillside, rise to the top corner of the field. On the far side of the gate turn left towards the left hand end house, across the road. Go over the stone stile and turn right into the hamlet of Taddington. In about 170 yards opposite the last farm buildings on the right, go through an opening into the field on the left. Follow the hedge and then a wall on the left to a point half way up the second field. Now strike diagonally right to a stone stile in a wall and so on to the road; turn right. Continue ahead with Stanway Ash Plantation on the left. At the end of this plantation a road comes in on the right. Go on for about a further 200 yards; here turn right up a definite track on the right of Welshmans Hedge Plantation.

400 yards up from the road the bridleway turns left through a gap in the wood to continue on the opposite side of the wood. In less than ¾ mile a road is reached. Cross this and go through the wicket gate opposite. In less than ½ mile go through a wicket gate into a thinly treed wood. Continue with the wall on the right and in just over ½ mile Hornsleasow Farm is reached. Here the path emerges onto a farm road near a cattle grid. The green lane opposite, which curves round to the left of the farm buildings, now leads, after 300 yards, to a metalled road.

Turn left along the road and the quarry from which the ramble began can be seen ¼ mile ahead.

Ramble 17
ICOMB,
MILTON UNDER WYCHWOOD

Map O.S. 163 in the 1/50000 series.
Starting point: Grid reference 213226 Icomb village.
Distance 13 miles. (The pub at Milton under Wychwood is 8 miles from
the start).

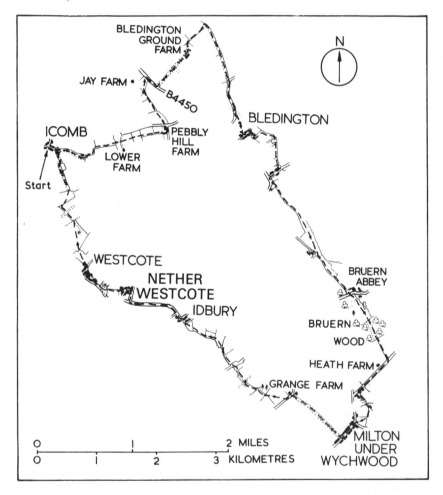

At the eastern end of the village pass to the right of the church along
a grass track, with some iron railings on the left, to a metal stile.

Turn left on the farm road and go along the track (sign-posted
Bledington) for ¼ mile to some barns. Pass to the right of the buildings

56

and in 50 yards go over the stile into the field. Turn left round the corner of the field and go through the gate (sign-posted Public footpath). Turn right along the hedge to the corner. Go over the stile and turn left and walk for 100 yards between a hedge on the right and some barbed wire on the left to a gate. Go through and continue over the next field with the hedge on the right. Keeping the same direction cross a narrow field to a gate opposite, on the other side of which is a farm track which to the right leads to Lower Farm. Cross the track and go over the field in the same direction as that taken across the narrow field and go through a gate into the next field. Keep the same direction and go over the wooden fence into the next field. Go over this field so as to arrive at the facing hedge a few yards to the right of some electricity lines. Go over the wooden fence. Now make towards Pebbly Hill Farm seen ahead. In the right hand corner of this field go through a gate and immediately turn left and go through another gate and cross the side of the field to gate opposite. This leads on to a farm track. Turn left to the road.

On the other side of the road slightly to the left, a gate leads into a large field. Ascend the field parallel to the hedge on the right. 150 yards beyond the highest point, go through a gate and then down the side of two fields to a tiny ditch stream. Go through the gateway and turn right, and with Jay Farm away on the left, walk with the hedge on the right about 20 yards away to a bridle gate near the middle point of the facing hedge and so on to the road (B4450).

Turn right along the road for 250 yards and left down the drive to Bledington Grounds farm. Pass between the farm buildings and a bungalow to bear left along a good track across a field. In 200 yards go ahead through the left of two gaps and turn right to follow the hedge on the right for ¼ mile to the bottom of the field. Here turn right and with the hedge on the left, continue for ½ mile across two fields. At the end of the second field go through the gate on the left.

Turn right along the track for nearly ½ mile to a point some 40 yards beyond an abandoned level crossing. Here turn left into a field and bear right to cross a stone bridge in the middle of the field. Keep the same direction to a small footbridge and through a narrow gap between cottages and so out on to the road in Bledington. (4½ miles have now been walked).

Turn left along the road for 300 yards to where the wall of a house seems to block the road. Here take the track right round the garden to a gate. On entering the field turn left to a small footbridge some 200 yards away. Before the footbridge, turn right along the bank of the stream.

Follow the stream to a wicket gate with a stile on its right. Go over the stile and follow the stream, now the River Evenlode, for ¼ mile to the main road (B4450). Turn right along the road for 300 yards and at the T-junction, turn left. In a further 100 yards on a sharp bend, leave the road by a gate on the left with an Oxford Way sign.

Bear right diagonally across a small field. Enter a large field and bear right and walk with a hedge on the right. At the end of this second field, continue in the same direction across a triangular field towards some cottages but leaving them several yards to the right. A coppice is reached towards the apex of the field. There is a track into the coppice about 80 yards before the stream at the apex. Go into this track and in a few yards turn left and walk through the coppice which is a nature reserve.

In ¼ mile the path emerges into the corner of a field. Continue ahead with a wood on the right to a wicket gate. Cross the road and go through the wicket gate opposite which has an Oxford Way sign.

Go ahead between the Bruern Abbey Gardens on the left and a cricket field on the right. Follow the boundary fence of the cricket field to a gate with a stile on the left. Go over the stile and continue in the same direction so as to meet the facing wood at about the middle point. Walk up the green ride. Looking back towards the restored house it will be se seen that the ride gives a distant view to those in the house. Keep to the left side of the ride and go through a gate in the top left hand corner. Pass ahead through the field, with a hedge on the right, to the road and turn right.

Passing Heath Farm on the right, go down the hill to cross a brook. At 150 yards beyond this point, a stile on the left leads to a path between gardens. After crossing a stream continue ahead to pass a cottage which is on the left. Immediately turn right along the left side of a hedge to a kissing gate in the hedge. Cross the recreation field diagonally to the road junction near the Quart Pot Inn in Milton under Wychwood. (8 miles have now been walked).

Go down the straight street for ¼ mile to the Baptist Church on the left, opposite which a track leads across fields for ¾ mile to Grange Farm. At the road turn left.

Walk along the road for 200 yards and turn into a field gate on the right by some electricity lines. Bearing left across the field pass over two stile/fences. Now make for the wicket gate, which is about 55 yards from the conifer wood on the right. Go through the gate and turn right. Follow the hedge which is on the right, and continue round the corner of the field for 20 yards. Go over the stile on the right and cross the ditch by a plank bridge.

Now follow the stream which is on the right to cross a concrete bridge and continue ahead on the opposite bank. Go through a wicket gate and continue across a small patch of pasture to a wide bridle path coming down from Fifield ½ mile away up on the left. A few yards to the left the path continues, still with the stream on the left, to a point about 120 yards into the second field. Here the main stream turns left. Cross the fence and drainage ditch on the left. The fence and barbed wire and deep ditch make this a most difficult crossing. It is hoped an improvement will be made. Go diagonally right across the field to the main stream and follow it round to the left and pass into the next field. Follow the river for about 200 yards further and then bear diagonally right to the hedge and cross this. (If the obstructions make it difficult to cross this hedge then follow it upwards to the right to the farm track. Turn left. Then in 150 yards cross the stile/fence on the right). Go diagonally right to a stile/fence at the left hand end of a stone wall. A track now leads to the main road at Idbury.

Turn left and follow the road round to the junction and take the road ahead to Westcote. In ½ mile take the first turning to the right through Nether Westcote. In 80 yards past the New Inn, the road bears left uphill but here keep straight ahead to drop down between farm buildings. In a few yards a spring on the left will be seen. This was the only supply to part of the village until recently. Bear left up to a stile and continue with the hedge on the right, over the three stiles and a rough waste, to emerge on the road at Westcote. Keep to the lower road past the church which is high up on the left. 200 yards past here, where the road bears left through the village, bear right. Turn left immediately beyond the last house and follow the garden wall which will be on the left. Keep the same direction across the field to a facing hedge. Follow the hedge to the right and round the corner and immediately go over a stile near a broken down stone wall. Go over a second stile. Cross the field diagonally to the bottom right hand corner and follow the track up the hill. Go over a bridleway and on into the corner of the field. Before going into the next field, turn right alongside the hedge for 100 yards and then bear left through the gap.

Bear right towards a point where a wood and a stream make a bow. This point is towards, but a considerable distance from the right hand corner of the field. Go over a footbridge and through a bridle gate. Now follow a path by a hedge which is the right and pass a small reservoir. A good farm road leads right round the farm buildings and so to the metal stile by the churchyard at Icomb.

Ramble 18
BOURTON-ON-THE-WATER, THE RISSINGTONS, THE BARRINGTONS WINDRUSH.

A ramble through typical Cotswold villages.
Map O.S. 163 in the 1/50000 series.
Starting point: Grid reference 172202 Bourton-on-the-Water.
Distance 13 miles.

Start from the car park opposite the cricket field at the south end of the village on the road to Little Rissington. Turn right out of the car park. Take the first turn left to walk with the playing field on the left. Go across a field with a hedge on the right. At the minor road turn right and in 200 yards follow the road round to a gate. Pass through and in 20 yards take a definite track on the right. There is now a quarry pond on each side (look out for heron and grebe).

At the end of the ponds follow the road round to the left. In 200 yards turn right across a tiny stream by a footbridge.

Veer half right across the field to a gate with a stile on the left. Go over the stile and continue ahead to the stream. Follow the stream to the right and go over two footbridges with the buildings of Rissington Mill on the left. Go ahead to the road.

Turn right. After passing through a gate the track takes a right hand bend. Here go through a gate on the left. Go diagonally right and make for a gap at the middle point of the facing hedge. Turn left and ascend to the top right hand corner of this field. Go over a stile/fence and then follow the hedge on the right to a wicket gate at the corner of the churchyard. Go through the gate and, with the church on the left, follow the footpath through to the church drive. Turn right to the road.

Turn left through Little Rissington. At the end of the village where the road makes a sharp turn left go straight ahead along a track. In 200 yards go through a gate and follow the narrow track next to a hedge on the right for 1 mile. At the bottom of the valley, where the track turns left keep ahead through two fields next to the hedge on the right to a wicket gate on the right in the corner. Go through and in a few yards turn left through a gate and go to the hedge on the right. Make for the farm buildings seen ahead and get onto the farm track to the right of these buildings. Turn left, then right at the sign post "The Barringtons". Walk through Great Rissington, taking the left hand turn, and near the Lamb Inn take the right hand road at the sign post "Village Only". Go downhill and turn left just before the post-box.

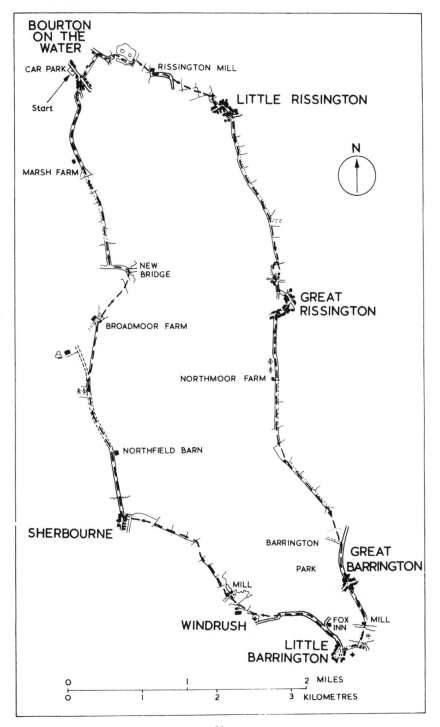

BOURTON
ON THE
WATER

CAR PARK

Start

MARSH FARM

RISSINGTON MILL

LITTLE RISSINGTON

N

NEW
BRIDGE

BROADMOOR FARM

GREAT
RISSINGTON

NORTHMOOR FARM

NORTHFIELD BARN

SHERBOURNE

BARRINGTON

PARK

GREAT
BARRINGTON

MILL

MILL

WINDRUSH

FOX
INN

LITTLE
BARRINGTON

| 0 | | 1 | | 2 MILES |
| 0 | 1 | 2 | 3 | KILOMETRES |

61

Follow this path for ½ mile to Northmoor Farm. After the farm buildings keep the hedge on the right for two fields; in the next field the hedge is on the left.

At the next field bear right downhill towards a stone farm building at the bottom of the valley. Continue up the other side with a hedge on the right to a track between two hedges.

Follow this track to the road. Turn right. Pass the cross in Great Barrington and go over the cross roads. When this minor road turns left continue along the bridle road past a mill and over a stream and follow a line of trees and shrubs on the left to a track in front of some cottages. Turn right onto a path into Little Barrington. (6½ miles have now been walked).

At the village green turn right along the road to Windrush. Continue ahead past the road on the right which leads to the Fox Inn. In a further 700 yards where the road turns sharply right, just before the village of Windrush, go over the waymarked stone stile. (From here to the village of Sherborne there are a complete set of waymarks but as it is not possible to see from one waymark to the next the following description may be helpful.) Make for some houses slightly to the left and continue ahead to Manor Farm which can be seen ahead. Alongside the farm go over the stone stile with a waymark and then follow the farm wall to the bottom of the descent. Here turn left over a wooden walkway and some stepping stones over a tiny brook.

Continue to follow the farm wall as it ascends to a gate and a stile on the left with a waymark. Go over and turn immediately right and go on with a fence on the right to a waymarked stone stile. Go over, then down the steps, cross the farm track, and go through the gate opposite marked Sherborne. Go ahead with the River Windrush about 50 yards away on the right to enter the next field through a gap and continue ahead with a fence/hedgerow on the left. Pass into the next field and go ahead with a fence/hedge on the left to a barn with a waymark. Pass the barn and go over a waymarked stone stile into the next field. Follow the hedge on the left; this leads to an open field. At the entrance to this field there is a waymarked post on the left. Follow the direction indicated by this waymark which means roughly the same direction and make for the electricity pole (waymarked) in the facing hedge (not the hedge on the right) and pass through the gap. Now walk with a hedge on the left over three fields with electricity poles going in the same direction. Go through a gate into a fourth field and keep in the same direction with a hedge on the right 20/30 feet away. Go over a waymarked stile in a fence and cross a field. Go over another stile, cross the farm track and go over the stone stile opposite into the outskirts of Sherborne village.

At a minor road turn right. In just over 1 mile there is a small conifer wood on the left. 200 yards beyond go through a waymarked gate on the right and then follow the hedge on the left to Broadmoor Farm. Follow the yellow arrows through the farm buildings and at a farm road turn right. At the end of the buildings where the road sweeps round to the right continue ahead along a waymarked path. In about 100 yards go into the field on the left at a waymarked post. Go in the direction indicated by the yellow arrow to the hedge straight ahead to a waymarked gate. Go through and then go diagonally left to a waymarked stile to New Bridge.

At the road turn left and in 300 yards take a bridleway on the right signposted. Go ahead over the field and in a few yards cross a farm bridge over a brook. Continue in the same direction, keeping parallel to the hedge and trees on the left so as to arrive at a gate on the opposite side of the field. Go ahead in the same direction along a fairly definite track but if there is any doubt make for the meeting of two hedges, one going to the right and the other straight ahead. Follow the latter to a gate. In the next field follow the track between two hedges and when these finish continue to a gate which leads into a field preceding a farm. Go across this small field to the left of a barn. Go through a bridle gate to the left of a gate on to a metalled track. Turn left and then go past Marsh Farm and then Marshmouth Farm. Opposite this latter there is a road type signpost pointing across the field which says 'Little Rissington 2½ miles as the crow flies'! This was puzzling until Mr. Medlicote told us there was no right of way and that the sign was erected in humour but the 2½ miles was correct. If you are lucky Mr. Medlicote may show you his very interesting collection of old farm implements and other items.

Continue ahead through Nethercote and on to Bourton. The car park at the beginning of the walk is on the left.

Ramble 19
NEAR BROCKHAMPTON,
SEVENHAMPTON, ANDOVERSFORD, FOXCOTE, PEGGLESWORTH HILL, WITHINGTON, SYREFORD.

A hilly ramble with fine views.
Map O.S. 163 in the 1/50000 series.
Starting point: Grid reference 047220 ¾ mile East of Brockhampton at a T-junction.
Distance 14 miles.

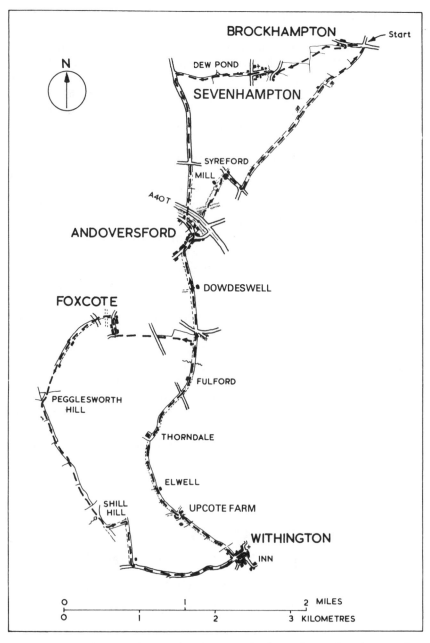

To get to the starting point from Winchcombe, take the road to Cheltenham. Just before leaving Winchcombe take a road on the left, signposted Brockhampton. Continue along the road for 3½ miles to a cross road with Brockhampton on the left. Turn into Brockhampton and continue for ½ mile beyond the village to a road on the left at the top of the hill. This is the start of the walk.

Walk back down towards Brockhampton for 300 yards. At the first house on the left which is at the bottom of a bank, go through a gate on the left against the wall of this house. Skirt the wall with trees on the right. In a few yards there is a stile in this wall. Cross this and continue westerly along the tree lined fence towards Sevenhampton seen below.

200 yards before the next field turn left in a south west direction up to a stile in the fence ahead. Go over the stile and keep the same direction over a field to a stile in the wall. Over the stile turn left and follow the wall round the right angle to a convenient crossing place 100 yards from the corner. Then turn diagonally right and go almost due west to the first building below. (This was the school). Go over the fence, cross the road and over another stile. Keeping the wall on the right descend to a stone footbridge then ascend to a road. This is Sevenhampton and do not hurry through it.

Continue to the road at the T-junction. Go over the road and through the gate opposite and with the wall on the left walk for 500 yards. Pass through the gate straight ahead and then walk with the wall on the right for ½ mile to the road. Turn left and follow this for a mile to another road. Cross this and go down the bridle path straight ahead. At the main road (A40T) cross over (traffic dangerous) and go straight ahead down a rough road through a yard to a road. This is Andoversford. Turn left passing the Andoversford Hotel which is on the left and at the main road turn right (A436). In about 200 yards take a pronounced bridle road on the left. In ¾ mile cross the main road.

Go along the bridle road on the opposite side. Pass through a gate and in a few yards at a storage barn turn right over the field and walk at a right angle to the bridle road just left. In order to check the direction, walk parallel with the hedge on the right. On reaching a hedge making a right angle, continue straight ahead to finish the crossing of the field with a hedge on the right. Make for the right hand corner and pass through a gap into the road. Cross the road and go through the gate opposite. Now follow the hedge on the right into Foxcote.

On going through the field gate at the beginning of the village turn sharp right. Go along on the right hand side of a wall. Continue through a yard and along a cartway, pass the farm buildings and in about 200 yards just at the end of the farm buildings and where the cartway swings to the right, go through a bridlegate on the left. Follow the hedge on the left, through a gate and straight across an avenue of trees and along the bridleway straight ahead. At the next road cross over and continue along the bridleway. Pass a barn on the right with some piggeries on the left. Continue in the same direction to a gate which gives entrance to a rising open field.

Go up the track ahead and as it levels out continue ahead to a stone wall. Here turn left along a definite farm track. Follow alongside a wall which is on the right for ½ mile and go through the gate straight ahead. With the wall now on the left, follow a line of pylons. Descend to a gate and go into a rough rising field. Bear slightly left across the field and pass a water hole which is on the right and still following a line of pylons to arrive at a wall on the left. Continue in the same direction to the corner of the field and go through a gate. Go ahead and descend slightly, with a line of trees on the right, along a rough track. (The Ordnance Survey Map may show a different direction for the path but this is the legal diversion).

When this track makes a T-junction with a rough road, with a gate a few yards to the left, turn right. In ¼ mile a subsidiary road is reached. Turn left and walk into Withington. The Mill Inn is down through the village. (8½ miles have now been walked).

Starting at the Inn and walking northwards, i.e. towards the church but not as far, take the first turn left and then the next turn right. Continue over the crossroads and follow the sunken bridle road through a spinney. On emerging from the spinney continue in the same direction for ½ mile through Upcote Farm. Keep straight ahead through the farmyard passing two cart tracks on the right and at the next fork bear right with a fence on the right. Continue for 1½ miles to Thorndale. Here bear right and continue along the farm track to the road. Cross the road and walk along the bridleway to Fulford Farm. Follow the farm wall on the left to a continuing bridleway and so to the main road.

Cross this road and a few yards to the left go along up the bridleway to A436. Turn right and then left into Andoversford. About 50 yards before the Andoversford Hotel turn right along a track through a yard. Go through a tunnel on to main road (A40T). Cross (traffic dangerous) and go along the metalled track ahead. With the sewage works on the left and a hedge on the right, continue to the old railway embankment. Turn right along the embankment and go through the dismantled railway arch on the left. Cross the field in front, keeping about 35 yards from the stream and hedge on the left. In about 200 yards at a large tree the hedge on the left comes round to near the path. At this point leave the path and go into the wood through an opening. This opening gets overgrown and is not easy to locate. Once having found it there is a clear path through the wood to a private road (with a public right of way). Turn right and walk to the road at Syreford. Turn right and at a fork in about 250 yards, bear left and almost immediately take a bridleway on the left. Follow this for 1½ miles to the beginning of the walk and completion of the ramble.

Ramble 20
CRANHAM COMMON, COWLEY, BIRDLIP

A varied ramble with woodland and high ridges giving good distant views.
Map O.S. 163 in the 1/50000 series.
Starting point: Grid reference 893131 Cranham.
Distance 15 miles.
(Note: The Green Dragon Inn at Cockleford is 9½ miles from the start).

To get to the starting point from Cheltenham go south west on the A46, the Stroud road. In approximately 6 miles pass over the A417 and continue for another 2½ miles. In a few yards past the entrance of Prinknash Abbey, which is on the right, turn left, signposted 'Cranham 1 mile.' In 100 yards, at a fork, bear right and in a little over ½ mile there is a parking place on the left, in a wood, with a Stroud District Council notice. This is the start of the ramble.

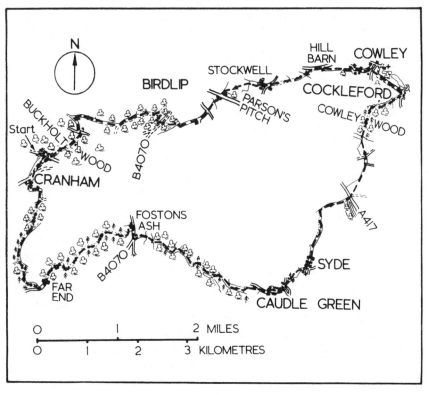

Go down the hill into Cranham village. At the bottom of the descent cross the tiny Painswick stream. 50 yards beyond the stream turn right. At the Black Horse Inn turn right and follow the sandy track. When the track forks do *not* follow the right hand green track but continue up the sandy track to the road. Go straight ahead along the road. Go over the cross roads up the sandy track and pass to the left of some houses.

In 300 yards the track turns left down to a farm. Pass to the left of the farm buildings and continue down to a stream: cross this. Do not go through the gate straight ahead but turn sharp right, ascend and go through a gate which leads into a sunken track and bear right into a coppice. At a point where there is a junction of tracks take the left hand ascending one and continue along this to a boundary wall nearly at the top of the ascent.

Follow this wall to the right to a facing gate. Do not go through this gate but follow the path to the right of it. In about 30 yards pass the gate which is on the left. In a further 10 yards bear right down through the wood.

At a T-junction with another track turn left and continue descending through the wood. On coming to other tracks keep bearing left. At a definite farm track continue ahead and follow it down to the road. Turn left. Go between the houses at Far End and follow the right hand waymarked track through Workman Wood which is a National Nature Reserve. Continue along this definite track for 1½ miles to the end of the wood. Cross a track and go through the facing gate which has a waymark. Follow the track to pass to the right of the building ahead and so to the road B4070.

Turn right along the road for 300 yards and then turn into the car park at Fostons Ash Inn. Go across the car park with the wall on the right to pass through a gate, and cross this field keeping near to the hedge on the right to another gate. In the next field bear right about 45° (compass bearing of 120°). This leads to a facing wood (Climperwell Wood). Enter this by a gateway and follow the definite track down through a gulley and so to a stream.

Cross the stream and turn right. Follow the stream until the track ascends to the left of the remains of some broken down walls and buildings. In a few yards go through a gate and immediately turn right. Follow the track back to the stream. Follow the stream for a further ½ mile. Just beyond a small lake there is a definite track to the right. Do not follow this but continue ahead and then where the valley sweeps round to the right, bear left up through a wood.

Pass through a gateway with a bridleway sign into a clearing and continue along the definite track with a wood on the right. In a short distance the track passes through woodland on both sides to a gate with a bridleway sign. Go through the gate and immediately turn left.

Follow the boundary fence which is on the left. At the corner turn right and follow the wall to two modern barns. Pass to the right of the barns. Do not go through the gate into the yard of the barns but continue alongside the wall to the first gate on the left. Go through to the road to descend into Caudle Green. 50 yards beyond the last cottage where the road turns right, go over the stone stile in the wall on the left. The path drops steeply to a stone stile in a wall. Go over this and ascend the road ahead with a house on the left, and in 100 yards turn right to pass to the right of a house. This leads down to a gate guarded by two giant Wellingtonia trees. Go through and continue up the track which veers to the right. Go through some farm buildings to a road at Syde. Turn left and in 100 yards left again.

Follow this road which soon becomes a track. Follow the track for ½ mile to where it ends at a gate. Turn sharp right (do not go through the gate) to follow a wall to a slip road. Cross thus, go over the bank in front, and continue ahead to cross A417T. Go into the entrance of the road opposite and go through the bridle gate on the left with a bridleway sign. Cross the field (compass bearing 30°) towards the wall directly ahead. Where, at a fence the wall turns sharp left go through a gate and follow the wall to a road. Go straight ahead and in 120 yards cross another minor road into the field opposite and continue in the same general direction making for the left hand corner. About 30 yards from the wood ahead, pass into the field on the left. Turn right and in 30 yards pass through a gate into Cowley Wood and follow the descending path.

At a T-junction (just before this junction there is a steeply ascending path on the right to be avoided) turn right. At the end of the wood continue ahead through the facing gate. Follow the hedge and wall on the left to the road. Turn left at Cockleford.

Walk up the road opposite the Green Dragon through Cowley Park. Just before Cowley where the road bends sharply right, continue straight ahead across the field with a fence and a line of electricity poles on the left. Towards the top of the field veer right to pass through a gateway. Go across the road and over the stile opposite. Proceed with a hedge on the right to pass over another stile into another road. Turn left.

In about 350 yards near some houses, the road takes a sharp right hand bend followed by a left hand bend. At the right hand bend there is a definite track straight ahead marked 'Hill Covert'. Leave the road and go up this track. In about 30 yards the track goes to the left. Do not follow it but go straight ahead up a minor track with a fence on the right and a wood on the left. Go over a fence and continue towards Hill Barn seen ahead. Go through a bridle gate and pass to the right of Hill Barn and then through a gate on to the road. Turn left and in 150 yards take a distinct bridleway on the left. Pass under some electricity lines and go ahead in the same direction up the rising field. Over the top of this ascent two enormous cylinders will be seen ahead. Make for a point about 100 yards to the right of these cylinders and continue to the road. Here turn left into Stockwell. At the first farm building on the left turn right into a road marked 'No through road'.

In 150 yards the road turns. Here leave the road and go through a gate on the left into a field. Turn right and walk with a wall hedge and trees a few yards to the right. At a facing hedge go over a stile into the next field. Cross this field veering left towards a prominent clump of trees seen ahead. On getting near the trees the general direction is about 70 yards to the right of them and this leads to a green track. Turn left and follow to the road A417.

Cross the road and go down the bridleway opposite. Follow this through a gate into a second field and continue ahead with a wire fence on the right to the road. Cross this and go down the road opposite. Where the road turns sharply left continue ahead along a distinct track. This track turns sharply right and then left. Follow the wall on the left for about 120 yards to where the track forks. Take the right hand track into the wood (compass bearing 286°) and follow it to the road. A careful check should be made to ensure that the right point on the road has been reached. Across the road straight ahead, a lake should be seen in the distance. Also in the wood opposite the descending footpath to be followed should be discerned. If there is still difficulty in locating this footpath then see that the point on the road is about 250 yards from where the road to the left forks. Take the descending footpath into the wood. In a few yards a wall is reached. Turn left along a definite descending track. In a few yards at a fork bear left. This descends gradually to a junction of tracks. There is one straight ahead which has the Cotswold Way sign (a white spot and a yellow arrow). Take this track for about ½ mile. During this ½ mile the track goes alongside a wall which is on the right. At one point the wall takes a right angled turn away from the track but comes back alongside the track later. At the end of the ½ mile there is a five-barred gate in a wall on the right. Take the ascending track opposite this gate to the road. Turn left and in 50 yards take a track on the right. Follow this to the right of a house named Monk's Ditch. Continue to the road junction in Cranham just before the telephone kiosk. Turn right and follow the road to the parking place in the wood.

Ramble 21
COMPTON ABDALE, FOSSEBRIDGE, NORTHLEACH

A fine ramble in the Chedworth woods area.
Map O.S. 163 in the 1/50000 series.
Starting point: Grid reference 061166 Compton Abdale.
Distance 16 miles.

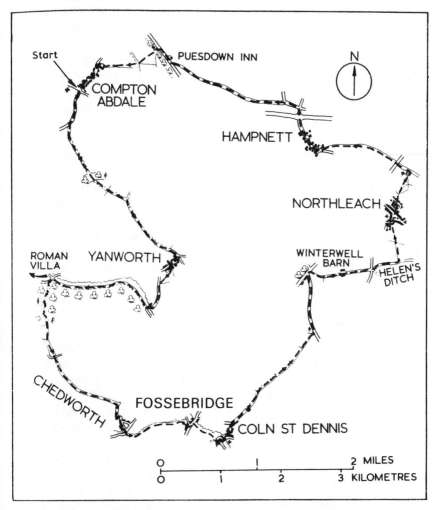

The start is at the cross roads in the centre of Compton Abdale. To determine the direction, stand at these cross roads with the road to the church on the right. Then ascend the road ahead. In 600 yards as the road levels out at the top of the hill there is on the left a double gate with a wicket gate and stile to the right of it. Go over the stile into the farm track and go ahead. At a junction with another track bearing left, pass through a belt of trees to the right. The bridleway merges into a good farm track and descends into Yanworth. Turn right at the road junction and in 200 yards turn left down an avenue of trees. At the bottom, on entering the field, bear right and so to the road. Turn left down the hill, past an old disused mill, and go over the River Coln to a sharp left hand bend. Here turn right and follow the metalled cartway with the river on the right and Chedworth woods on the left, for 1 mile. At the junction with the road, turn left and in 100 yards take the bridleway on the left to enter the woods.

In about 50 yards there is a track on the right but ignore this and continue ahead along a more definite track. In a further 300 yards there is a fork. Do not take the path to the right but take the ascending one immediately to the left of this. Continue through the wood. On emerging from the wood through a gate continue along a track with a wall on the left to the corner of the field. Do not go over the stile in front, which provides a descent into the valley, but bear slightly left to go through a wide gate on to a track. Proceed past a stone farm building and in a short distance cross a road and follow the track ahead. At a point where there is a gate into the field ahead and a grass track goes to the left, turn right down the bush lined cartway. Take the first road on the left to a junction with the road at Pancakehill. Turn right and at the bottom of the bank, where the road turns right, go through a gate on the left into a field and follow the path with the stream on the left for ¾ mile to A429. (7 miles have now been walked).

On entering A429 turn left for about 100 yards and opposite the Fossebridge Hotel go over the road and over a stile into a field. Walk with the river on the left for ½ mile to Pindrup Farm.

Go to the right of the farm boundary wall to a farm road. Go through a gateway on the opposite side of this road, and cross the small field with the farm buildings on the left, to a stile. Cross the private garden (there is a right of way) and go through the garden gate to the road. Bear left into Coln St. Dennis. Cross over the river bridge and take the first turn left to ascend the road immediately facing the church going north. (The memorial plaque in the church is interesting inasmuch as it is in memory of those who were spared as well as the fallen in the 1914–18 war). In 250 yards where the road turns left, take the track on the right and follow this north for 1½ miles to Saltway Barn.

At the road turn left and in ¾ mile at A429 turn right, and then in 30 yards go through a gate on the right to take the green bridle road with a wall on the left to a gate. The track becomes a road past a small farmhouse called Winterwell Barn.

At the next road keep straight ahead taking the grass track known as Helen's Ditch (not the drive on the right to Cats Abbey Barn).

Just beyond the end of the first field on the left, turn left and with the wall on the left after 300 yards, emerge into a meadow overlooking the playing field at Northleach. Keeping the same direction, cross in front of the pavilion and bear left on to the road. Here turn right and follow the road to the square in Northleach. This beautiful church, largely perpendicular, has some very interesting brasses. The modern furnishings are designed in perfect taste and are the product of Russells of Broadway.

Compton Abdale
The Crocodile's Mouth

Leaving the square by the bottom left hand corner at the war memorial, cross the road and go up the narrow lane opposite to a housing estate. Turn left and in 50 yards turn right along a path between house gardens.

At the next road turn left, and at the end of the second house on the right, turn right through a garden to a stile. Continue ahead to a second stile. Over the stile veer to the right and in 30 yards go through a gate on the right. In this field follow a line of hawthorn trees. Where the line of hawthorns bear right, continue ahead making for a point about 100 yards to the right of the farm seen ahead. Go over the fence on the right in the corner of the field. Turn left and walk with a wall now on the left to a stone stile. Go over into the definite track, turn left and continue to the road A429.

Take the track on the opposite side to Hampnett which can be seen ¾ mile ahead slightly to the left.

At the road turn right to go through the village of Hampnett with the church on the right. Continue ahead for ½ mile to A40. Cross this and go up the road opposite. In 70 yards turn left signposted Hazleton. In about 350 yards, where the road turns right, leave the road and go up the bridleway straight ahead. Keep straight ahead to the Puesdown Inn on the A40.

Turn right for 200 yards and, crossing the road, pass through a gate immediately before the Honey Pot restaurant. Bear slightly right across a field to a gate in the facing wall. Go across a farm track and through the opposite gate. A line of cottages will be seen ahead slightly to the right. Go across the field towards these to arrive in the corner of the field at a stile. Go over the stile and continue with a wall on the left to the end of a short road. Turn left down into Compton Abdale.

Ramble 22
LAVERTON, FORD, PINNOCK, STUMPS CROSS, STANWAY

A ramble with fine ridge views and packed with interest.
Maps O.S. 150 & 163 in the 1/50000 series.
Starting point: Grid reference 073357 Village of Laverton.
Distance 17 miles.

With the school on the right go up the road, and at the end pass through a gate. Follow the rising definite track ignoring the indefinite tracks to the right and left, for approximately ½ mile. In the course of this ascent look backwards at the fine view including the charming setting of Buckland Church.

A T-junction with another track is reached where there is a line of beech trees. Here turn left and descend to a gate. In ¼ mile beyond this gate there is an upright stone pillar. Here leave the track and bear diagonally right across the rising ground to a point between two woods.

Go through a gate and follow the farm road with a view of Snowshill across the valley on the left. Continue along this road for over 1 mile to a T-junction. Turn right. Walk for ½ mile along this road to a parking space on the left overlooking an old quarry. Here turn left and go along the long straight road with the old quarry on the right.

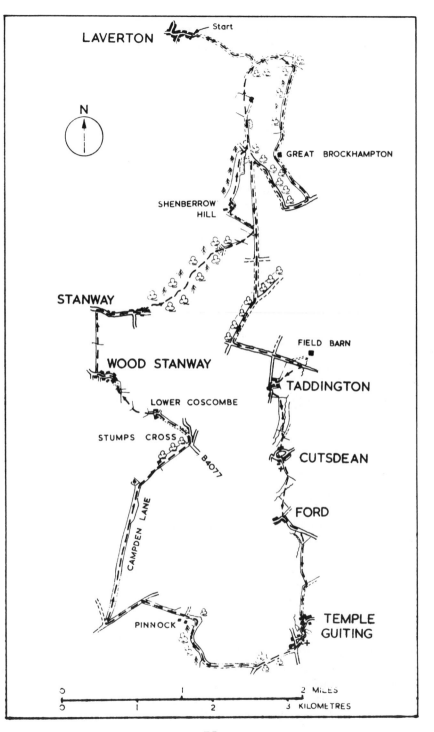

In ½ mile there is a definite farm track on the right but continue straight on. In a further 250 yards go through a bridle gate and over the cross tracks. In a further ⅓ mile go through the narrow Stanway Ash Plantation to the road.

Bear right along the road and in less than ½ mile turn left downhill, and go straight over the cross roads. In 250 yards a track leads off left to the Field Barn Farm which is the source of the River Windrush. Continue beyond this for a further 150 yards to the bottom of the descent. Turn right through a gate. Bear right across the field towards a large green cylinder and to the left of the stone barn seen ahead. Go through the farmyard and out on to the road. This is Taddington.

Turn left along the road for 100 yards to just beyond the last cottage on the right. Here turn left over a stone stile. Veer right to a gate. Through this, go round the hill dropping to a stone bridge over the River Windrush, and then rise up on the other side to a gate a few yards above the stream. Continuing round the hill for a further 20 yards, the path rises steeply to a kissing gate. Go through on to a farm track. Turn right and in 100 yards ahead, go through the left of two gates into a farmyard, and then through another gate on to the road at Cutsdean.

Cross the road and go over the stone stile opposite. Cross the paddock to another road. Ahead and to the right of a house a track leads into a field: then with first a wall and then a hedge on the right, in 250 yards turn right through a kissing gate. Keep near to the right hand hedge for 100 yards and then drop gently down to a kissing gate through which a stream flows. Veer right up the bank in front and continue to a facing wall. Go through a gap in the wall and continue in the same direction making for the buildings seen ahead. Pass through a kissing gate onto the road opposite the Plough Inn at Ford. (6¾ miles have now been walked).

Turn left along the B4077 road. In 400 yards turn right over where a partly tarred track has been made across the verge and pass through an iron gate into a small rough field. Incline diagonally left to the corner of the field, go over the fence and up into the field. Follow the hedge which is on the right and over which can be seen the valley of the Windrush. In 400 yards pass through a wide opening to a T-junction with a farm track. Turn right to Temple Guiting.

At the road turn right to go downhill over a bridge and up to a sharp right hand bend. From this road you may see Muscovy ducks and moorhens. Just after the bend an opening on the left leads to the church which is 13th century (restored) with a 17th century tower. 5 yards along this opening, opposite the end of a house, a gap leads through a coppice. When the path emerges onto the road, go up the lane opposite. In 500 yards, just over the crest of the hill, turn right along a bridleway overlooking Guiting Wood on the left.

The track follows the hill round to the right to drop gently and then swings round to the left to the farm at Pinnock.

Cross the farm drive and go through the gate opposite. Keep to the hedge on the left to a sunken track. Follow this to the road. Turn left, and in 600 yards turn right into the Farmcote road. In a few yards there is a fork. Leave the Farmcote road by taking the right fork which is the Campden Lane, an old medieval salt way, for 1¾ miles to the B4077 at Stumps Cross (note the stump).

Turn left and immediately left over a stile signposted Cotswold Way and Wood Stanway. Proceed in the direction indicated by the signpost along a definite track. Continue to follow waymarked posts indicating it is the Cotswold Way (a yellow arrow and a white dot). Descend to a waymarked gate and stile. In the next field go to the waymarked post and then veer right to a stile which gives access to the field on the right. Now follow the waymarked posts to a wicket gate and stile. In the next field follow the indefinite track to pick up further waymarked posts and descend to a stile giving access to a farm track. Turn right and follow the track into Wood Stanway.

Just beyond the last building on the right, turn right along a well-defined footpath to the road near Stanway. (12 miles have now been walked.)

Turn right up B4077 to a sharp right hand bend. Here continue straight ahead for a further 50 yards to where a road merges into two bridleways. Take the left hand one and climb through Lidcombe Wood. Continue through the wood, avoiding the "Private Paths" on either hand, until the farther end of the wood is reached. Go through a gate incline slightly left with the edge of the wood on the left, to a handgate marked "Bridleway to Shenberrow and Snowshill". Cross the cultivated field, inclining slightly right to a gap between a hedge on the left and a wall on the right. Go through and continue in the same direction across a cultivated field to a gate in the right hand wall and so on to a stony track. Turn left, and immediately left again along a bridleway. The bridleway leads round leaving some cottages on the left in a paddock, and through some farm buildings to an iron gate. Go through, and turn right. Note the outlines of the British Camp. Continue along a clear farm track for ½ mile. At the iron gate go through on to the road. Turn left and in 12 yards turn right along a rubble track. Pass through a gate into a field. In about 300 yards, the main track forks right to Laverton Hill Barn. Do not take this but fork diagonally left across a field for 250 yards, and pass through a gate. Continue along a definite track, gradually descending for 400 yards, to where there are a number of beech trees on the right. Here turn left down the sunken track, this being the track followed at the beginning of the walk. Descend into Laverton.